SESAME STREET, PALESTINE

SESAME STREET, PALESTINE

Taking *Sesame Street* to the children of Palestine: Daoud Kuttab's personal story

BearManor Fiction

2018

Sesame Street, *Palestine*
Taking Sesame Street *to the children of Palestine:
Daoud Kuttab's personal story*

© 2018 Daoud Kuttah

"Sesame Street" is a registered trademark of Sesame Workshop

All rights reserved.

For information, address:

BearManor Fiction
P. O. Box 71426
Albany, GA 31708

bearmanormedia.com

Typesetting and layout by John Teehan

Published in the USA by BearManor Media

ISBN — 978-1-62933-249-9

To Yasmeen, Saleem and Dalia, my three grandchildren born in Jerusalem. I dedicate this book to them in the hope that they can enjoy and learn from Shara'a Simsim.

Table of Contents

Acknowledgements ix

Introduction 1

Sowing the Sesame Seed 3

Taking the Plunge 11

An End at the Beginning 23

Tiberias, the First Gathering 29

Pre-Production Underway 39

Photos 56

Israelis Visit with an M16 63

Smuggling and Filming in Tel Aviv 71

Crossovers: Putting Israelis on a Palestinian Street 79

Arrest and Hunger Strike 89

Epilogue: Overcoming Obstacles and Jumping Hurdles 107

Acknowledgements

LIKE ANY PUBLISHED WORK, *Sesame Street, Palestine* would not have seen the light without the support and encouragement family and friends have given me. My four children: Tamara, Bishara, Tania and Dina have always been the drive in bringing *Sesame Street* to Palestine and have always been my supporters and my inspiration.

My wife, Salam, who became a mother of four within one year of our marriage, has been my rock and my fortress. She has given unlimited support and space and has encouraged me every step of the way.

This project was nothing more than an idea until I met Lucy Cripps at the International Press Institute World Congress in Vienna. When I asked Lucy, who edited a lot of the IPI publications, if she was willing to help me turn my idea into a published book, she enthusiastically agreed and has been my greatest supporter, and a top-notch editor, who has humbled me in the process.

Lucy's enthusiasm and encouragement to dig back through my memory for yet another story and another anecdote has helped make this book the hopefully enjoyable and readable publication it is. She gets all the credit for its success, and I take responsibility for any of the book's weaknesses.

Family and friends both on my side and on Lucy's have been so regularly corralled to read excerpts of this book that this acknowledgment would not be complete without giving them their due.

My nephew Jameel Brenneman, who helped me discover Bear Manor Media, which focuses on books about television, deserves special acknowledgment. Ben Ohmart, BearManor Media's publisher, immediately responded positively after tens of major publishers passed on the well designed and written proposal Lucy and I had worked so hard on.

Introduction

This is the story of making *Sesame Street* in Palestine. While making a children's television program is usually an apolitical act, this was extremely political.

The story takes readers into the politics, finances, and nuances of bringing an American television production to the children of Palestine. It deals with and documents the ups and downs of the peace process, and how it affected us: From the assassination of the Israeli Prime Minister Yitzhak Rabin a day before the inaugural curriculum workshop to the U.S. government's sudden funding cessation for the fourth co-production because of the results of the 2006 Palestinian parliamentary elections.

While this story tells the politics of Palestine, Israel, and America in relation to the co-production, the book also reflects on internal issues of the newly established Palestinian National Authority and its lack of tolerance of political dissent.

Sesame Street, Palestine is a portrayal of the passion and desire of Palestinians, young and old, to be free of occupation and enjoy life in an independent state.

1 Sowing the Sesame Seed

I AM USED TO EXPECTING the unexpected, but the call from the producers of *Sesame Street* totally surprised me. I was so unprepared that I nearly walked away from what would be one of the greatest opportunities for me personally, for my television organization—Jerusalem Film Institute—and for the future of Palestine's children.

As an English-speaking Palestinian journalist living in Jerusalem, I am not short of opportunities appearing out of the blue. This one, however, caught me off guard because it was not a straightforward political news story, news feature, or documentary, but an idea for a children's television program.

I am not sure exactly how the Children's Television Workshop in New York knew about me, or where they got my phone number, but, one day early in 1994, I had a call from an Israeli PR woman:

"Mr. Kuttab? Daoud Kuttab? Hi! Roberta Fahn, I represent the Children's Television Workshop—the *Sesame Street* people. One of our senior producers, Dr. Lewis Bernstein, is in Jerusalem and is very keen to meet you to discuss an opportunity. Are you free to meet us at the American Colony Hotel in Jerusalem for lunch?"

When my parents emigrated to the U.S. in 1970, I was too old for the iconic preschoolers' TV program, but it was impossible to live in New Jersey, or anywhere else in the United States, and not know Big Bird and *Sesame Street*.

The call certainly intrigued me, so I agreed to meet with them. Regardless of what I knew about *Sesame Street* in America, I had moved back to Palestine and had children exactly in the target age group of the world-famous show. My children, like all Palestinian children at the time, rarely saw entertaining and educational children's programming. Neither of the two television channels that we had access to at the time—Jordan TV and Israel TV—provided any age-appropriate programing, leaving us to use VHS tapes of Western children's shows, which they simply watched over and over and over. So, for sure, I was excited to hear whatever this Dr. Bernstein wanted to talk about—maybe even television programming for our children—but I was also worried about the politics.

I readied myself as I arrived at the American Colony, a popular, accessible spot for meetings between Palestinians, Israelis, and foreigners in Jerusalem. I found it funny to meet at the luxury hotel to talk about Big Bird and *Sesame Street* when I knew how closely the hotel was connected with the Oslo Accords—it was here that the initial phase of the secret negotiations took place in 1992.

As a regular visitor to the Colony, I was greeted by some of the Palestinian waiters on my way to one of the blue-and-white tile-topped metal tables in the courtyard. To the sound of the water fountain, Roberta Fahn introduced me to a representative from Israel Educational Television and a bearded American man—Dr. Lewis Bernstein.

As I sat down, an incredibly optimistic Dr. Bernstein introduced me to the ideals of the Children's Television Workshop and explained how this pioneering project, then in its third decade, was—and still is—a work in progress. He shared the *Sesame Street* story: How Jim Hensen, Joan Cooney and others had attempted to harness the power of television to provide under-privileged children in the U.S. with some basic preschool education.

When the waiter came, Dr. Bernstein ordered the popular Arab salad, mezze, (I later found out that, as a devout Jew, he orders salads whenever he is unsure if the food is kosher). For my part, and without being sensitive to the fact that religious Jews do not like the mix of dairy products with meat, I ordered a cheeseburger. Dr. Bernstein never made anything of it. On my recommendation, we shared a pitcher of Palestine's popular *laimon w nana,* lemonade made from fresh lemons and crushed mint.

As we broke bread, Dr. Bernstein insisted, "Please, call me Lewis."

Lewis punctuated his presentation with jokes and anecdotes as he enthused about how the Workshop provided so much more than just cognitive skills (it took a while before I understood that the word 'cognitive' meant teaching children things like the alphabet and numbers). It was about life skills, like sharing and respecting others.

Sipping at the mint lemonade, he worked hard to help me understand the power and the excitement of a *Sesame Street* program. He explained the parallel pillars of education and entertainment as the foundation of any *Sesame Street* production; about how children in their formative years need to be entertained and excited as they learn.

"Honestly, Lewis, this is music to my ears," I said. "I have seen first-hand how flawed our educational system is, and I love that television could be harnessed to educate Palestinian children. They could do with some fun and excitement in their learning."

As he spoke my mind often wandered to my own children, Tamara (nine), Bishara (six) and Tania (four), who along with their friends and school children across Palestine would benefit greatly from such an exciting television program. This was all like a dream come true. The whole reason I had gotten into television in the first place was to educate and inform and highlight the Palestinian narrative, and it looked like this could tick a lot of boxes. But the next words out of his mouth brought those dreams crashing back down again.

"We're proposing a regional version of *Sesame Street*. It will attempt something much more ambitious than anything we've done before. Something to coincide with what's happening here politically—the Oslo Accords and all that. This is a region in change, and we want to help children deal with that change. We want a production that could bring together Israelis and Palestinians working towards mutual respect and tolerance.

"Israel Educational TV wants a Palestinian production company to create authentic Palestinian segments to place in their show, and, maybe, over time, expand that out to being your own broadcast."

Wearing his Jewish skull cap, he talked, trying so hard to convince me to take the leap of faith. He wanted me to believe that having lived in Israel and attended Hebrew University, he understood the area and its sensitivities, but that he was still able to look at this project as a neutral American. "It would be a people-to-people project, improving understanding and relationships on and off screen between Israelis and Palestinians."

Lewis told me about a series he produced called *Shalom Sesame* and told me of the episode in which his own daughter appeared with the famous Mary Taylor Moore, his daughter making fun of the world-famous actress trying to learn a few words in Hebrew.

"With children leading the way," he explained, "anything is possible. Political borders can be non-existent."

As a Palestinian father, I was captivated, excited, and caught up in his rose-tinted enthusiasm, but as a Palestinian patriot, I was worried about the political cost of such an adventure. As a true believer in dialogue and nonviolence, I wanted to take a chance, but as a realist, I knew Palestinians, who had been living for decades under Israeli military occupation, would not accept it, and the political cost of such an idea was too big for me to take on. Palestinians suddenly becoming friendly with our occupiers in an innocent children's program? It was too fast and too big of an idea. Without much discussion, I said no.

Palestinians learn early to roll with the punches; you learn to adapt quickly to survive. Even as a child from a comfortable family, I saw daily struggle and witnessed the devastation of war first hand. On the eve of the 1967 war, my parents were away, so with my brothers and sisters, alone and scared of being caught up in the fighting, I scurried to our aunt's house in the center of Bethlehem, abandoning our rented home near Rachel's Tomb on the outskirts of the city. Sure enough, shells broke through, but, thank God, our home was empty.

In our refuge, a makeshift hospital, the war-injured lay in agony; I saw bodies ripped to pieces come through the door. My aunt, from my father's side, whose husband had died in 1948, was working as a staff nurse at the nearby King Hussein Hospital. She had seen the decapitated body of a young boy and rushed home screaming, terrified that it was my older brother, Jonathan; she ran through Bethlehem's streets and smothered him in kisses when she found him safe at home. Someone else's tragedy was our relief.

As I dashed around helping as best a twelve-year-old could, I worried whether my school friends in Jerusalem had survived the shelling. One good friend, Hatem Nusseibeh, lived just ten minutes' walk from the Damascus Gate, where there was heavy fighting.

The violence reached deep into Bethlehem. Just as the 1967 war ended, with Israel occupying the west of the Jordan River, I was watching from my aunt's house as our neighbors across the street given minutes to evacuate before their home was razed to the ground because Israel had accused a member of the family of being part of the Palestinian resistance to the Israeli occupation. Seeing that family hurry from their house with what possessions they could grab was scary, and I remember it to this day when I hear and see news of houses demolished and families ripped apart as Israel takes land deep in Palestinian territory. Years on and Israel's creeping occupation still makes even the simplest things in life a challenge.

Despite growing up under occupation, I have become a true believer in dialogue and nonviolence, and as I sat facing Lewis, I was familiar with public diplomacy projects. I had even participated in dialogue groups with Israelis during the previous years. I was cognizant that the current peace process had started as people-to-people negotiations. In fact, I pointed out room sixteen to my guests: The room, which overlooked the courtyard we were sitting in, was where the Oslo Accords all began.

Despite Lewis's valiant charm offensive, I was not budging in my stand against bringing a version of *Sesame Street* to the Middle East. I was impressed with Lewis' passion, but I was opposed to the concept and the timing. "I am all for the ideas that nurture mutual respect and tolerance, but this is not the top priority for the Palestinian people," I said.

"What we are witnessing now," I argued, "is the beginnings of negotiations for a Palestinian state. The entire thrust of the Palestinian people—whether at an official or unofficial level—is creating the environment that will usher in our long-awaited independent homeland."

To try to persuade me, Lewis turned to an example we both knew and understood well: the long battle for civil rights in the States. He argued that *Sesame Street* had motivated generations of U.S. children to accept, even enjoy, the differences in the cultures that exist in their melting-pot country. I responded by telling Lewis that our situation is different from the American model.

"This is just not the case in Palestine. We and the Israelis have no unifying constitution. What we have here," I told Lewis, "is a case in which a battered spouse wants a divorce rather than marriage."

I continued the divorce analogy to illuminate the plight of the Palestinians. "Following years of abuse and discrimination as Israel and Palestine have attempted to live a false and unequal relationship of occupier and occupied, we want this relationship to be over. We want an end to the agony and the fighting. Any hopes of legitimizing our marriage with Israel are folly. Our number-one goal, as Palestinians, is to build up and strengthen our own, independent national identity."

To make my point of view clearer, I emphasized the difference with South Africa and the U.S.: "The situation in Palestine is different from Apartheid South Africa, or even the American Civil Rights Movement. For people in both countries, the goal was equality and integration. We are looking for an amicable divorce that will allow us to go our own separate ways as independent states, living side-by-side." I explained that Palestinians crave a secular, democratic state shared by our two peoples, but while Israel is not interested in a multi-national state, Zionists insist that they want a state as Jewish as France is French or Britain is British.

The Oslo Accords had, at that time, begun the process of ending the Israeli occupation, with the aim of separating us into two independent states. Although the Oslo Accords had given this process a five-year interim period, the fact that Israel and the PLO recognized each other and vowed to end the military occupation, which had begun back in 1967, was the best proof that Israelis and Palestinians, at least for the near future, had chosen separation rather than integration.

Applying the issue to our *Sesame Street* discussion, I argued that the idea of a joint Palestinian—Israeli television program for children was the last thing we needed.

"It is not that we are not interested in helping children nurture the concepts of respect and tolerance, but our priorities as an emerging nation are much different. We need to show our children that we—and they—can control their own narrative.

"If this high-quality, expensive project gets off the ground, it will overshadow any other children's program we produce ourselves. And we won't even have our own television station until the Oslo Accords come into effect. Imagine the reaction if the very first program on our new national television station was a joint Israeli—Palestinian program.

"There is no way that the Palestinian leadership, the new team running Palestinian TV, or even the Palestinian public will accept or tolerate having our maiden program on our own national TV as not wholly Palestinian."

Lewis smiled: "Nothing is etched in stone. There really would be no problem with the Palestinian team identifying its own priorities, even if the number-one priority was pride in culture and language. At the moment, the funding is for a co-production, but that's not to say we're dismissing the notion of a separate project with Palestine TV. A program totally Palestinian in looks and in content."

It sounded OK, but I was not convinced, nor did I believe that they were serious ideas, but Lewis was not giving up either.

"We are planning to do this project with Israel Educational TV, no matter what," he concluded. "I would still love to have you as a partner, but if you choose not to accept our offer, I would like to ask a favor. We are determined to include Palestinians in this project, whether on an organizational level, or on an individual level. This is a great opportunity for your people and for your creative community. If you know animators, actors, or any other creative talent that would like to participate in this project, we will be happy to work with them. This could be an amazing training opportunity, and they could forge a career with the experience we'll give them."

Lewis and his Israeli friend both gave me their business cards and, as we shook hands, implored me not to let this opportunity pass. I thanked them and we parted ways.

2 Taking the Plunge

AFTER MY MEETING with Bernstein, on the way back to work at the Jerusalem Film Institute (JFI), I walked past St George's School, memories of childhood, my last days in Jerusalem and the first days at school in New Jersey playing over in my mind.

Halfway through my tenth grade at St George's School, after a couple of years living under occupation following 1967's *an-Naksah (set back)* war, my parents' U.S. emigration papers arrived, and we left Jerusalem rather quickly. While my school mates had little time to adjust to my departure, they did not miss an opportunity to goad me by speaking in English. They said they were doing it to prepare me for when I was 'surrounded by people who only spoke English and didn't know any Arabic.' But my English was as good if not better than my Arabic, so their taunting did not bother me.

Although we all had the Israeli-issued Jerusalem-resident ID card, which gave us considerable freedom of movement in areas under Israeli control, in December 1969, Mom and Dad had us living in both Jerusalem and Bethlehem when the emigration papers came. We left Palestine and went to Amman, Jordan, to stay with our uncle, before our flight left for Cairo, then from Cairo, we flew KLM to Europe and on to the States.

I remember that flight vividly: I had a window seat, though all I could see were clouds. When the pilot said we were approaching Amsterdam's Schiphol Airport, I did not believe him. But seconds before landing, as soon as the plane broke through the clouds, the landing strip appeared; I was so impressed with the pilot and the plane's navigation.

Within days of arrival in the U.S., I found myself a junior starting at Snyder High School in Jersey City, New Jersey. My Aunt Nada, who had welcomed us into her home in the U.S., told my parents that the high-school curriculum in Jerusalem and the Middle East is much more intense than in the U.S., so she had entered me in eleventh grade, a grade above what I'd been doing in Jerusalem.

At fourteen, I had very little understanding of the new land and new culture that I found myself in. I saw a different way of life in a country free of barriers, a world away from the one I grew up in. During my teens, all I wanted was to be like all the other high-school kids: to speak American, to think American, to be all-American.

Although I was far too old to be interested in watching, I was vaguely aware of a new preschoolers' TV show—*Sesame Street*—which launched around the time we arrived. I remember stumbling over the crazy monster puppets when I was channel-hopping, trying to find the action-western *Bonanza* TV show while Dad was out. My dad, a Christian pastor, was not too impressed with any TV or cinema, but my relationship with media—visual and printed—started early.

In another step to become more American, in my spare time and to help my family financially, I took a newspaper delivery route and was assigned two streets, including our own street. On the paper route, I got bonuses for getting new subscribers, which motivated me to get family and friends to take Jersey City's local newspaper, the *Hudson County News*.

Here I was once again, in 1995, trying to make sense of two worlds trying to come together. Deep in thought, I took five minutes to get from the American Colony to our Jerusalem Film Institute offices in the street behind the world-famous hotel. When I walked into the office, I ran into Ayman Bardaweel.

"Morning, boss!" Ayman was one of the talented young artists I had met during JFI's well-received animation workshop in Ramallah a couple of years earlier, and he was doing some volunteer work with us. Ayman, the son of a school teacher in Gaza, had studied and trained as a civil engineer at Palestine's leading university, Bir Zeit, but, luckily for JFI, wanted more creativity in his work.

"Morning!" I said to Ayman, absent-mindedly. "Oh, hey, if you're looking for animation work," I handed him the two business cards I had just received, "there's an opportunity to work on a project in Tel Aviv with the *Sesame Street* people. You could improve your animation skills and make some money as well." Ayman's mouth dropped open, his eyes widened, bewildered, and his hands flew up:

"What? Why isn't JFI involved?"

I gave him a summary of what I had heard from and said to the Americans and the Israelis and told him that this project was not for us as an organization, but that he should feel free to work with them; "They seemed nice," I told him.

"Wait, wait," urged Ayman, "do you know who this is? This is *Sesame Street*. Why are you giving up on a once-in-a-lifetime opportunity? I never dreamed that they would be coming here. Can you please reconsider?"

I was adamant: "This is not for us; it's not politically right for us, as a leading Palestinian organization, to get into this 'dialogue with the other side' issue. Can you imagine the reaction to it? You're from Gaza; you know what people will say. They'll accuse us of selling out our cause for a few American dollars. And with whom? With the mainstream Israeli Education TV. This is the station that spews out propaganda against us, calling Palestinian fighters 'terrorists' and daily besmirching our cause. You want us to go to the lion's den and work with them? You've got to be kidding."

But Ayman was not going to back down. "Let's think of ways for our role to be autonomous. Consider how we could do things our way. Please, I want to be in this project, but not alone. Don't leave me alone with these people in Tel Aviv, they'll eat me alive.

"If we go in as an organization, we can make certain demands. You know how to deal with these Americans; you could make changes to prioritize our national needs. We can do this without giving up on our cause, and we can make this benefit our own children. Imagine if they can see *Sesame Street*-quality programming instead of the rubbish that they see every day."

Still reluctant, I decided to go see George Khleifi, my friend and business partner. George and I worked well together, balancing each other out. We complemented each other. He, for example, gave himself title of Artistic Director, while I went for the pompous role of President. George made things happen in the organization, working hard to implement our plans and execute them, while I was the public face, taking on the fundraising and public relations.

Growing up in Nazareth, George was an avid supporter of the Communist Party and later Rakah, the Democratic Front for Peace and Equality. He had little time for religion and for anyone espousing religious beliefs, often making fun of people of faith—of all faiths—and trashing their holy books as works of fiction. But he knew the books and used them to counter religious fanatics from all faiths in our region. But, still, his irreverence often bothered me, a devout Christian.

What drew me to George was his attitude to art, his experience and knowledge, especially in TV and films, and his genuine interest in true peace. George would be a sure bet against joining the *Sesame Street* project, I thought.

But George was not supportive of my position, either; he saw merit in the project, too. He had always hoped that Palestinians would shift from boycotts and anti-normalization attitudes towards Israelis and instead adopt a campaign to change Israeli attitudes from within.

"This project can help us influence the Israeli mainstream. What better way to do it than through their own national TV station?" he argued.

And using his own flowery language, George admitted that some militant artists, and others, would attack us and try to present our effort in an unpatriotic way:

"But f**k them. All they do is talk. Anyways," argued George, "this would be a perfect learning experience, a chance to counter the prevailing Israeli stereotype of Palestinians, and at a minimum, we can use the project to train an entire generation of creative talent."

Maybe George was right; many Israelis maintain that Palestinians are uncivilized and generally not as cultured as the European Jews. They say Palestinians do not love their children because they allow them to protest the occupation.

Maybe I had jumped the gun when I totally rejected the idea. But how could I go back to Lewis and the Israeli team? How could I reverse my earlier argument about our need for an amicable divorce? What would our relationship look like? Would I be able to negotiate, as Ayman had suggested, better terms?

Reluctantly, I got the business cards back from an excited Ayman, picked up the phone and asked to speak to Lewis. I invited him to come alone—without the Israelis—to our East Jerusalem offices. He agreed.

Lewis came without his *kippa,* the Jewish skull cap, and accepted my offer to make him some hot tea with *meramia.*

"I think the English word for *meramia* is 'sage.' Our parents and grandparents still tell us how therapeutic it can be, but I really just enjoy it as tea!"

Lewis, also keen to show his willingness to engage, sipped the *meramia* and listened as I told him about our Jerusalem Film Institute and our ethos. I wanted him to understand where I had been coming from in rejecting his offer—so maybe we could find some way to make a Palestinian *Sesame Street* happen.

"Years ago," I began to explain, "I was involved in a government-driven media technical committee tasked with coming up with practical ideas that could be applied should the peace talks produce some kind of political breakthrough. We decided that, as a nation in waiting, we should be ready to create our own national Palestine TV station. Our lack of experience and knowledge put us on the backfoot, but we got a grant from SIDA, the Swedish aid agency, and we ran a two-week broadcast-news workshop in the Palestinian National Theater in East Jerusalem.

"We trained Palestinian talent to create, produce, and present a thirty-minute mock news bulletin to be broadcast in the theater hall on closed-circuit TV at exactly 6 p.m. Alongside the studio-based interviews with Palestinians of opposing political views, the program had culture, art, and local sports, and closed with Palestine's weather report, superimposed on a map showing the West Bank and Gaza.

"I took the tapes of the show on a speaking and fundraising tour in the U.S. in the hope of raising serious money for the potential Palestinian Public Broadcasting: A broadcasting company that would be very different to the government-run Arab TV.

"Things moved quickly," I continued, "and soon, from his exile headquarters in Tunisia, Yasser Arafat issued a decree appointing a twenty-six-person committee to set the foundation for Palestinian broadcasting. I was chosen, along with many of those from the experimental workshop, including one Radwan Abu Ayyash, as part of the committee.

"It didn't take me long to realize that Abu Ayyash's concept of a public broadcasting varied greatly with mine, and while I travelled in the U.S., Abu Ayyash called a meeting of the twenty-six and elected a smaller steering committee of five to start the day-to-day planning of the Palestinian Broadcasting Authority. From that moment and for many years to come," I said to Lewis, "the tiny administrative group, headed by Abu Ayyash, took charge and that was the end of my part in the Arafat-appointed committee."

Lewis nodded and sipped more *meramia* tea. Clearly, he could begin to see where I was coming from. I continued.

"I had never wanted to be part of any governmental or semi-governmental organizations, so I turned to providing young Palestinians with proper broadcasting training and workshops through the Jerusalem Film Institute, which George and I set up in 1991. The publicity we'd gained from the experimental news workshop gave our institute a big push, and we were able to get more funding for a practical, hands-on training program.

"My trip to the U.S. also proved successful. A number of donors, including George Soros's Open Society Institute, generously supported our effort to prepare the very first generation of Palestinian television broadcasters. With the funds, we converted part of the Palestinian National Theater into a television studio. We created a control room overlooking the studio and began a three-month intensive training program that again ended with a simulated broadcast of a news show. Many of those involved in the experimental workshop, and the subsequent long-term training program, have become leading anchors in Palestinian and some in Arab television stations.

"Life at JFI is never dull. For the first time in Palestinian history, at our annual film festival, Jerusalem Cinematic Nights, we screened films made by well-known Palestinian film makers living in the diaspora. With their Western passports, they could go to the major international film festivals, but none of those festivals came close to their excitement of seeing their films, which dealt with the Palestinian cause in one way or another, shown to Palestinian audiences in Palestinian towns: Ramallah, Nablus, Bethlehem, Hebron, and, of course, Jerusalem.

"Our focus and ethos is and always has been Palestine TV for the people by the people. And we've made it our business to make the most of our unique residency in Jerusalem and our ability to travel freely to other West-Bank towns to connect with Palestinians living under occupation.

"Take the town of Beit Sahour, the home of the Shepherd's Field in which Archangel Gabriel announced Jesus' birth to the shepherds: Denied travel permits, the mainly Christian—Palestinian people of Beit Sahour can't get to Jerusalem to celebrate Easter, so we decided to take Easter to them. We created an outdoor show on the eve of Easter Sunday. With help from the local municipality and the Orthodox Club, we took our TV equipment, hired a large screen, prepared a few TV features covering Easter events in Jerusalem and invited the local people to a fantastic outdoor extravaganza. And you know what, nearly the entire town came out. We had a local anchor interview people in the crowd to add to the fun. The event remains strong in their and our memory. It was Palestine TV for the people by the people, and that's what we're about—and that's why I worry so much about joining the Israelis."

Lewis often nodded as I talked. With *Sesame Street* broadcast on public broadcaster channel thirteen in New York, he applauded my vision of keeping government away from television production. But he was a realist and understood quickly that his ideas for *Sesame Street*, as nice as they were, were unlikely to work in the messy Middle East.

I told Lewis that, while my political point of view had not changed, my colleagues had persuaded me of the importance of this project to us as a people, as a nation, and especially for our children.

I knew he had already talked to many people and organizations, so I was concerned we would be outflanked by others, making our efforts in controlling and managing this project difficult at best, and totally useless at worst. Pouring another sage tea, I told him that we—the Jerusalem Film Institute—would be willing to discuss it if he was willing to accommodate our needs.

Lewis leaned back breathed out and opened his arms wide: "Listen, I will do as much as I can to make this partnership work."

"We'd have to be the only Palestinian party involved, and for us to work together, it would need to be on a basis of trust and exclusivity. And we'll only work with the New York-based Children's Television

Workshop and not with the Israeli Educational Television. Even if we coordinate with the Israelis, it's important that everyone understands who our relationship is with." I was stunned when he agreed immediately, so I pushed on.

"A high priority for us is training. We'd need good-quality trainers from the U.S. to support us, and generous budgets allocated for training. We'd want this project to help us create a Palestinian cadre that will operate long after this project is over."

Lewis leant forward and furrowed his brow, "The budget we're working with now has a fairly low amount set aside for training. But I agree a heavy dose of training is needed to get the talent up to the quality of a *Sesame Street* production."

My heart leapt. In principle, we had come to an agreement. *Sesame Street* was coming to Palestine. And I was keen to get started. "So, what's next? What's the first step to making this happen?" I ordered in a late lunch of falafel, salad, and pita, and we rolled our sleeves up, turning our focus to content and the goals of the project.

"It doesn't matter to us how small our *Sesame Street* is; we just want to end up with Palestinian Muppets and segments that can be shown on TV or on video to Palestinian children, regardless of the Israeli—Palestinian component."

"Understood," said Lewis, "but you need to come at this now from the child's point of view. What messages do you want to give the children? The next step, really, is to lay out criteria that will drive the project, the elements that will dictate *Sesame Street* Palestine's success."

"I guess our number-one goal is to make sure the children watching it must feel good about being Palestinian, whether from a cultural or political point of view. We need to nurture pride in our national identity, culture, and language," I said, seeing the reality of what lay ahead.

"And goal two would be to develop respect for our culture and the Palestinian environment," I postured, but I was not talking about a green program; we wanted our *Sesame Street* to reflect Palestinian life, community, and topography. But this was probably the hardest point to deal with: Do we show evidence of the Israeli military occupation or simply ignore it? While we wanted the program to be rooted in reality, I was adamant that to keep the program evergreen, we should not deal with temporary issues such as the Israeli occupation—especially with the 1993 Oslo Accords signed, the end of a forty-six-year war agreed, and a real feeling of hope with liberal, peace-focused Rabin as Israel's prime minister. It was also not a good idea to push politics down our children's throats at such an early stage. I clarified our second goal with "we need to be rooted in reality but be positive and forward looking."

Then Lewis drew my attention to our need for *Sesame Street* to introduce preschoolers to early-years' education. "What I know of Arabic, there are several dialects, aren't there?" said Lewis, "What language will you use for Palestine's *Sesame Street*?"

"For *Shara'a Simsim*?" I joked, using the Palestinian dialect for *Sesame Street*, "that's easy. It has to be in colloquial Arabic—it's the best way to reach children."

Literary Arabic, Fusha, is the written and official version of Arabic, spoken during news programs and officials' speeches. It is very different to the language spoken at home.

Understood by all Arabic speakers regardless of their geography or colloquial variation, the classical language sounds weird when you use it with children, and certainly would not work for a dialogue between Muppets or between Muppets and humans.

Hearing dialogue in classical Arabic is like hearing people chatting at a café using Shakespearean English.

"How art thou today?"

"Thou hast many ideas to express."

"I beseech thee, help me with mine ordeal."

Obviously, you understand the message, but it does not engage children. But to appeal to the widest possible audience, many Arab TV producers use standard Arabic to overcome the range of dialects used from Iraq to Morocco, UAE to Lebanon. What happens, though, is they lose their audience.

I knew that in insisting we use colloquial Palestinian Arabic, we would risk backlash from Fusha-orthodox educators, who would want to see *Sesame Street* contribute to children's mastery of the Arabic alphabet and language, but we wanted the program to be further ranging than just language acquisition and development.

"That makes sense," said Lewis, "and to counter any criticism, you can produce an alphabet song and other animated shorts to improve children's language skills. Great!"

With three goals settled, we leaned back, both reaching for some pita, falafel, and hummus.

"So how did you find being a Palestinian in 1970's America, if you don't mind my asking," said Lewis, cutting through business and reaching out personally.

"Ha! It was a challenge. I started high school within days of arriving in December 1969. Having my aunt right there made it a bit easier, but I wanted so much to be a part of American life, to be that all-American kid, but was always reminded of my upbringing, of who I was, and where I came from the moment I stepped foot inside our strict Protestant New-Jersey home. I learnt quickly to integrate at school and to enjoy very different freedoms to the ones I'd seen back in Palestine. Women with equal rights, a clear acceptance of the other—of me—and girls in school."

As we talked of our experiences living and learning in Palestine, Israel, and the U.S., both similar and vastly different at the same time, another goal revealed itself.

"You know what, it's those notions of tolerance and mutual respect that I saw so often growing up in the States that we need to see more of here in Palestine. By opening up channels of communication with children, we could start to see a more open, tolerant society within a generation," I said, getting excited about the future.

"Wouldn't that be something?" said Lewis. "So let's set respect for 'other' as your fourth goal. There's no question it's been a successful goal Stateside, and, let's face it, the more people know about the world, and how other people, cultures, societies, and races function, the better, and the closer to peace we'll be."

Lewis was right, of course. And in an ideal world I would have agreed with him. But Palestine, however near peace was in autumn of 1995, was not an ideal world, and we had a long way to go before we even came close. Palestine had too much to fix internally before it was able to look out.

"No. We can't put others before ourselves."

Lewis was clearly taken aback by my statement, so I explained that we needed to give priority to issues of pride in Palestinian culture and language, showing respect to our own communities and encouraging mutual respect within our own society. When we could achieve that, and only then, could we discuss and engage in showing respect to the other societies. I wanted to make sure that we could deal with 'the other' from a position of strength, and not as an imposed idea coming from rich New Yorkers who see our conflict as one in which they can experiment at will, without taking into consideration the opinions of the indigenous people.

Listening as he loaded another pita with more hummus, falafel, and salad, Lewis smiled, clearly amused by my 'rich New Yorker's comment, "You're absolutely right. Let's come back to 'other' later, then. But I think you've stumbled across your fourth goal: tolerance and mutual respect within Palestinian society." This time, he was right.

Even though Palestine is small and relatively homogeneous, *Sesame Street* could tackle the intolerance of the female within our society; tackle city people's intolerance of Palestinians living in rural areas or who live in refugee camps. I wanted mutual respect to have its own Palestinian—Palestinian component and was happy to have that as our fourth goal, leaving the fifth goal to focus on respecting 'the other,' whether that was Israel or Japan or America.

I wiped away the last of the hummus with a bit of falafel, all the pita gone, then sat back in my chair and smiled at Lewis. I could tell that Lewis liked my toughness and engaged well with it. Together we were going to lead a project that had been highly improbable just a few days earlier, and a project that many—including me—had thought was naive and worthless.

In the weeks and months that followed, we had lots of discussions, late-night phone calls during which we exchanged many ideas, some which failed and most which succeeded. Lewis's attitude and desire to learn and engage with me and the rest of JFI was felt and welcomed by all as being genuine and honest. He made an extra effort to learn about us and our national aspirations; he would often call or email saying he had read something I had written about the conflict and wanted to discuss it. While we sometimes talked politics, for the most part we did not need to—our focus was on bringing *Sesame Street* to Palestine and helping the next generation understand each other and move away from conflict.

Lewis's sincere efforts to reach out, I believe, paid off on all sides. Lewis and I have a wonderful friendship which stretches beyond the confines of our offices and into our family life. Although our politics are different and our upbringings poles apart, we are grown-up versions of what JFI and Children's Television Workshop want to achieve through *Sesame Street* in the Middle East.

3
An End at the Beginning

AFTER SOME NUMBER CRUNCHING, Lewis called me at the office a couple of days later to tell me he would be able to set aside $300,000 for training:

"That includes trainers coming from London and New York to Jerusalem to train us in filming, animation, and directing, and for us to go to New York for an orientation meeting," I told smiling faces at JFI after the call.

"Fantastic! And to think we so nearly had nothing to do with *Sesame Street*!" laughed Ayman.

The office had a real air of excitement and anticipation; we were all looking forward to heading to Tiberias the next morning for the three-day curriculum conference that happens at the beginning of any of Sesame Workshop's international co-productions. In just a few hours, at Beit Gabriel Guest House on the banks for the Sea of Galilee, we would meet the American and Israeli teams and start to get our heads around our new joint venture.

But the feeling of hope was not all down to *Sesame Street*. Hope is a strong part of the Palestinian character, and even after decades under Israeli occupation—losing homes, land, and family—hope across the territories was riding higher than it had been for a long time in that fall of 1995.

There was the promise of the Oslo Accords opening the negotiations for a true Palestinian state, and, in the meantime, we had had self-governance in Palestine, however limited, for a couple of months already—the biggest step in decades towards a recognized sovereign Palestine and peace between our two nations.

Driving home through the relatively deserted streets that evening, I could not help but feel positive. I pulled up next to our home in Qalandia and pushed through the gate. The children's toys were still on the ground under the tree after a hard day's playing, and Nuha was sitting on the terrace in the evening quiet, looking out across Qalandia refugee camp.

Nuha Abu Alis and I had met through friends in Bethlehem—I had meant to be meeting her sister Hilda, but Nuha's confidence and warmth drew me to her instantly. We talked a lot and found we had much in common: We had both been educated in the States, though under significantly different circumstances. When her father died, Nuha had travelled with Hilda to the U.S. to finish her last two years of high school. Nuha, like me, was not what people expected of a child from a conservative Palestinian family. Unlike many Palestinian women at the time, she worked—and enjoyed the independence that her work gave her.

We were a good match, and, on her condition that she could continue to work, which I was totally fine with, we married in Jerusalem in 1984 and honeymooned, after a boat trip riddled with her sea sickness, at a family friend's summer home on the Greek island of Patmos.

We had wanted to wait before having children, but in the spring of 1985, we found out Nuha was pregnant at the same time as her sister Judith (we call her Juju). My brother in law, excited about the pending arrival of his first child, promised to hold a feast if he had a son.

"Why would you throw a feast only if you have a boy?" I had asked. "You know what? If we have a daughter, I'll hold a feast."

So, shortly after September 13, 1985, when Tamara was born, I threw a big *mansaf* (a feast of rice, hot yogurt, and lamb) in our large apartment in the Jerusalem neighborhood of al Ram. It was soon after that that we moved to our home in Qalandia, just north of Jerusalem, where both our son, Bishara, (named for Nuha's father Annuncio and the Spanish for Bishara) and daughter Tania were born, in a hospital literally across the street.

Years later, on my way from Jerusalem to the office in Ramallah, I took a detour to see the comfortable two-story apartment we had lived in between 1988 and 1997. When I passed down streets I had once recognized, I found that the refugee camp and town of Qalandia, now famously home to one of the most notorious Israeli checkpoints, had grown so much since the year that *Sesame Street* had first entered my life that I could barely find the apartment. Gone was the view, gone was the quiet serenity, all replaced by high-rise apartment blocks, squashed together to house the growing population of Palestinian refugees forced out of their homes in 1948 and needing more space.

That November in 1995, though, we were happy there, and life was good, with Rabin and Arafat set to bring peace to our part of the Middle East, and hope hanging in the air.

No one could have known how the events of that evening would affect change in Qalandia, in Palestine, and across the Middle East.

After kissing the children goodnight and enjoying a meal with my wife, I clicked on the TV, muted it, and booted my laptop, so I could write as the world around me slept. Thoughts of everything new I would learn in the workshop the next day kept me awake.

Searching for the right word in my article, my eyes rested on the muted television. Through the flickering, I realized the film that had been on was replaced by commotion. A yellow 'breaking news' tape scrolled across the screen in Hebrew, under footage repeated over and over: Israeli soldiers and security personnel were pinning a young man against a wall. This was not the usual Palestinian—Israeli stuff. The guy being pinned did not look Palestinian, and, while the security people were making sure that he did not escape them, they were not hurting him in any way.

The phone rang next to me, and a journalist friend told me that the young Israeli against the wall was Yigal Amir. He had just shot Israeli Prime Minister Yitzhak Rabin. My friend hung up, pulled away by the story. I turned my full attention to the television, but my Hebrew is not strong, and the images were not changing enough for me to guess what was happening. With one eye trained on any changes in the story, I returned to writing my column, but my mind wandered.

Rabin. His power and belief in peace had inspired hope in the Middle East and promised change to thousands of Palestinians and Israelis. But he had also had a direct influence on my life, personally. I glanced at the photo on the wall of Rabin and me on the day of my ground-breaking interview with him in June 1993. It was my big journalistic break, and all I had done was apply the first rule of journalism: I had asked for an interview. Simple.

Although, to be fair, it was not that simple. No-one had attempted this kind of interview before. As a journalist working for the widest-circulating Palestinian newspaper, *Al Quds*, I was no novice, but when I suggested the idea of a Palestinian reporter interviewing the Israeli prime minister, I expected to be scoffed at. But with the go-ahead from the founder and publisher of *Al Quds Daily*, Mahmoud Abu Zuluf, I called up the Israeli prime minister's office and asked for the interview. Sometime later a low-level Israeli official called me and asked, "Where will you publish the interview?"

"In *Al Quds*, Palestine's number-one daily," I answered, and he swiftly set up the appointment. I was excited and nervous, all at once. For a Palestinian journalist, interviewing the prime minister of Israel—and having that interview published in the leading paper—was potentially political and professional suicide.

My hour with the prime minister arrived. I said 'hello' as I was told to sit. Following a cold response, I suggested we start the interview—there was apparently no room for small talk here. For sixty minutes, we conducted the interview, in English; the photographer took a few pictures and when the interview was over, Rabin simply walked away. I had uncovered no political breakthroughs, and, apparently, no personal ones either.

But Rabin's reaction to one question left me puzzled. I had asked: "You are talking to Palestinian leaders chosen by the PLO, and the Palestinian organization is giving the negotiators regular directions, and receiving feedback from them, when will you stop this game and just talk directly to the PLO?"

I must have caught the Israeli prime minister off guard. Rabin turned to one of his aides and muttered, "How can I answer this in a nice way?" The aide pulled out a cigarette and lit it up for his boss. Rabin puffed a few times before he gave a stock answer about preferring to not negotiate with terrorists.

Why had he drawn on such a neutral, meaningless answer—and why would he want to answer in a nice way? It turned out that almost at that very moment, Rabin's own delegates were holding secret talks with the PLO in the Norway's capital, Oslo, so his enigmatic answer had been designed to not scuttle these talks.

The photo on the wall looked down at me as I remembered Rabin and watched the rolling breaking-news footage of uniformed and non-uniformed security surrounding the young Yigal Amir at the Tel Aviv peace rally. That interview had changed the course of my career, putting me on an international stage, and, although I did not know it yet, Rabin was once again going to push me back into the public eye.

Shortly after 11 p.m., a shaken up Eitan Haber, Rabin's spokesman, stepped out of the hospital and made a statement in Hebrew:

"The government of Israel announces in consternation, in great sadness, and in deep sorrow, the death of Prime Minister and Minister of Defense Yitzhak Rabin, who was murdered by an assassin, tonight in Tel Aviv. The government shall convene in one hour for a mourning session in Tel Aviv. Blessed be his memory."[1]

The Israeli Prime Minister and figurehead of the Oslo Accords, and the peace process had died from the wounds inflicted by a Jewish assassin.

Next day, *The New York Times* reported one woman as saying: "I'm not crying for Rabin, I'm crying for Israel," in the same article they explained "The rally had been called by a coalition of left-wing political parties and peace groups as a response to increasingly strident street protests by the right-wing opponents of the peace agreement. More than 100,000 people turned out on Kings of Israel Square in front of Tel Aviv's city hall; organizers declared it the largest rally in the coastal city in at least a decade."[2]

Moments before he was mown down, Rabin and his Foreign Minister Shimon Peres had closed the emotional peace rally with a rousing peace song. Flags waved, smiles ruled, and hope hung in the air. Rabin moved among well-wishers, smiling, and shaking hands. As he was escorted to his car, still holding the words of the peace song in his hand, three shots rang out above the cheers, and Rabin crumpled to the ground. The blood-soaked peace song sheet endures as a metaphor for the man, the process, and the hope that died in that moment.

On the one hand, I was relieved that the killer was not Palestinian, but at the same time, I wondered how Rabin's death would affect the peace process. This was a political earthquake. My understanding

---

1. Ministry of Culture and Sport (in Hebrew). 2010-12-29. היפרגוויב – ויבר קחצי *[Yitzhak Rabin – Biography]*. Retrieved 2015-05-06

2. Assassination in Israel: the overview; Rabin slain after peace rally in Tel Aviv; Israeli gunman held; says he acted alone, By SERGE SCHMEMANN, November 5, 1995, *The New York Times*

of the peace process gave me an advantage in predicting how Rabin's assassination would play out politically, even though I had not entirely understood the Hebrew newscast. That the assassin was an ultra-right-wing Jew, I believed, would turn most regular Israelis against the radical few: and especially against settlers and their messianic ideology.

As we woke to a post-Rabin world and waited to see how each nation would react in the peace negotiations, our Sesame curriculum workshop was postponed for the national day of mourning on Sunday; so, on Monday, we made our way to the-then fairly new guest house and cultural center in Tiberias.

4 Tiberias, the First Gathering

OVER THE COMING MONTHS and years, political restrictions on both sides meant that the Palestinians and Israelis would meet only occasionally, and the first curriculum meeting was overshadowed by one of the most significant setbacks to peace in a long time. Rabin's assassination. In 1995, his murder had taken us from being a region on the brink of peace to one where hopes of a brighter future were shattered. Two days after the assassination, after a three-hour drive into northern Israel, passing through just one checkpoint, we arrived at the hotel on the shores of the Sea of Galilee for the three-day curriculum meeting.

We started with solemn handshakes and half smiles, and much of the talk between the Palestinian and Israeli teams was of the assassination, trying to come to terms with the circumstances. For both Palestinians and Israelis, emotions were high as we explored and discussed the repercussions of the assassination, and where hope could come from next. But many of us are moderates, believers in nonviolence, and we found ourselves more committed than ever to the co-production, returning to our project fired up and ready to go. Maybe we could offer hope, maybe *Sesame Street* could help the next generation grow up with a greater sense of respect for self, and for what is right. It would start by our being able to finally break the decades-old TV portrayal of Arabs being camel riders, thieves, and terrorists.

To break us in gently, Lewis explained the fundamentals of Muppet design. He explained that we needed to think through everything connected to our future Palestinian Muppets. From nature (animal, human, or monster-like) to the color, features, and personality, and how we could portray everything the Muppet stood for to our viewing audience.

Adamant our characters should challenge ethnic stereotypes as successfully as the Israeli's *Street* did, we had a free-talking session to explore Palestinian and Arab stereotypes to get our creativity moving. George Khleifi, the drive behind most of the characters and their descriptions encouraged us to think of stereotypes that we would like to change. I pointed out that we are often accused of always being late for meetings, appointments, and public events. A famous Syrian comedian once began his show thirty minutes late, saying that he and the other performers had been ready on time, but "out of respect for the Arab tradition of tardiness" they had decided to start late.

Stereotypes can be funny, of course they can, but the aim on our *Street* was to break through those stereotypes. By using a comical stereotype, we hoped to amuse our preschool audience and give them a new moral code and higher standards to strive for. After chuckling our way through a range of stereotypes, we landed on it. A loud rooster, a visual metaphor for punctuality. Karim, our boy rooster Muppet of six years old, needed to be so passionate and so obsessed with time that he would wake the other characters up, even on weekends, and ensure the residents of *Shara'a Simsim (Sesame Street)* arrive punctually for everything.

As with any excitable character, Karim needed someone to spark with, so we dreamed up Hanin, a confident red girl monster of four, who would live up to her name, which means gentle, smart, and beloved.

We tried to begin pulling together the basic sketches of Karim and Hanin, but it would be several months and many tweaks and changes to color, attribute, and shape before we saw them come to life. For the time being, though, we were happy to have made such strides so quickly.

Next morning, over a table of tea, coffee, and refreshments, we turned our thoughts back to our core values, the values Lewis and I had agreed on over tea at JFI a few weeks before: To inspire children to feel good about being Palestinian, culturally and politically; to develop respect for our culture and the Palestinian environment; to engage Palestinian children in their spoken language; to nurture tolerance and mutual respect within Palestinian society; and, finally to learn how to respect 'the other.'

This was the bit I was excited about. This was where we would have autonomy to explore our culture. Lewis explained that we should "make a show that was fun for Palestinian children, one that they would be proud of, and one that would widen their horizons without taking away from their national and cultural identity."

"Tell me," Lewis asked us, "what are Palestine's national and cultural icons and symbols? When you've worked that out, we can start sketching out the ten crossover segments, where Israelis and Palestinians appear on the Street together."

Ayman looked at the table piled with food to keep us going: "Hummus? Pita?" he ventured, a cold laugh rippled around the room with a flicker of resentment from the Israelis at the table. Israelis claim both foods as their own, a stand which, over the years, has caused nearly as much tension between our peoples as their systemic hijacking of Palestinian land and homes.

But I had barely heard Ayman. All that rang through my head was Lewis's ridiculous suggestion that we create ten crossover segments.

"Ten?" I said, maybe a little louder than I had meant to and amplified by the sudden tension in the room. "Ten? Are you kidding me? How are we meant to contrive ten occasions Israelis and Palestinians meet? It's unrealistic. It's not a natural representation of the world our audience lives in. We'd not just need to cross cultures, but languages, and huge political divides—ten times. That really will be very difficult."

"Maybe we should not focus on how many we'll do. Let's keep our focus on Palestinian icons and symbols for now, and just see where the discussion takes us." Lewis stepped in, smoothing over two rifts in one. "I appreciate this is delicate, but we all need to find a way to make this work."

He was right. Now was not the time to get emotional. I poured some water and dipped pita into the hummus, "Well, Ayman is right; there is the food of the region," I said, smiling. "Sure, we all claim it as our own, but that could be something worth looking at. Later."

We sat in silence for a few moments; Palestinians thinking about our culture and all it means to us. And then a memory of me as a child hit me; I was sitting and watching my grandmother pick up her needlepoint.

"Embroidery!" I said, to surprised giggles. One deep-rooted aspect of Palestinian culture is our embroidery. "My grandmother liked nothing more than sitting down to some needlepoint; it was wonderful to watch her create intricate designs. It was mesmerizing."

"Tell me more," said Lewis, keeping the conversation moving.

"I like it," added George, our Artistic Director. Turning to Lewis, he took over, "Palestinian women pride themselves on their embroidered dresses, each one unique to their own town or region. My grandmother was the same, and I have such strong memories of watching her create the most beautiful patterns. If we can work out how to make something that had appealed to us and our grandmothers come alive for a new generation of children, we could be on to something."

As everyone discussed the possibility of inspiring children with embroidery—especially the boys—I heard Ayman say quietly, "The keys to homes taken over by new Jewish immigrants, which we pass from generation to generation." Then, as if pushing a memory aside, Ayman looked up: "What about olives and olive trees," he said to the room. "And lemons. *Maqluba*—an upside-down casserole—falafel, fattoush, shawarma, baklawa." Laughter grew around the room as we listened to Ayman, apparently unaware of our discussion about embroidery, build his hit list of Palestinian delicacies as the afternoon turned to evening and the end of our first *Sesame Street* workshop drew to a close.

"Ayman, you've made me hungry," Lewis chuckled, and we settled down to our first meal together.

As the workshop went on, it became clearer that there had to be two separate programs, one Palestinian and one Israeli. Politically and personally, we knew we would need interactions between the two sides, but how to bring the two nations on our *Sesame Street* together in the crossover segments was too big a challenge with the death of Rabin so raw. Ultimately, we left the crossovers for a later meeting, mainly using the curriculum meeting to exchange general ideas about how to use television to promote peace, tolerance, and mutual respect.

During the discussions, we learned the Israeli team wanted their program to reflect the diversity of the Israeli population, so they wanted a black Falasha (Ethiopian Jew) character, as well as an Arab character. The term Israeli Arabs appeared at one point and Nizar Hassan, a respected filmmaker who comes from a village near Nazareth, explained that "Arabs living in Israel are also Palestinians, as much as Palestinians from the West Bank or Gaza."

Then Nizar really put the cat among the pigeons: "Since 1947, Palestinians have been planted in their towns and communities, whereas most Jews, including the Falashas, who were airlifted to Israel in the Eighties, have chosen to emigrate to Israel of their own free will. Israelis are brought up believing the conflict they are dealing with is somehow an internal problem, that Palestinians are in revolt for national reasons and not because they are trying to improve their social status. There is little willingness among many Israelis to deal with Palestinians as a separate national group with political needs rather than as an internal Israeli problem."

True. But while few Israelis of the time repeated Golda Meir's infamous rhetoric of 1973 when she asked "Who are the Palestinians? There are no Palestinians," many Israelis still struggled with the Oslo Accords, which had given national identity to the Palestinians of the Occupied Territories. And here they were, a day after their leader was assassinated, hearing that they must deal not only with the Palestinians in the areas occupied in 1967, but they should recognize the national rights of citizens within their own country.

Nizar stood his ground: He insisted the Israelis and Americans in the production teams use the term 'Palestinian Israeli' when referring to any Palestinian characters they wanted to introduce in the Israeli program; they were also to use characters that would break stereotypes. So instead of Palestinian—Israeli characters having menial jobs, they should be professionals: doctors, lawyers—journalists. He even suggested that if the Israelis were feeling especially courageous, they could create a professional female Palestinian role. Even though we were all being mindful of not developing onscreen relationships, they liked the idea. And as a result, they created in the Israeli program the role of a female doctor, a character called Amal, which means 'hope,' played by a well-known actress and singer of the same name.

With such liberal, forward thinking appearing in the Israeli camp, we were motivated to explore ever-more exciting ideas for our own *Sesame Street*. Primarily, our storylines and characters needed to focus on pride in culture, pride in language, and pride in nationality. Initially, exploring Palestinian—Palestinian respect needed to take priority over Palestinians building relationships with Israel. But as we chatted, we saw barriers lowering and a mutual respect appearing between us. It was clear that even though none of us was talking in our native language, everyone—Palestinians, Israelis, and Americans—was relaxed and comfortable in the shores of the Sea of Galilee.

Each day, we crammed in as much as we could, breaking only for coffee and cigarette breaks during working hours, and in the late evenings, many of us walked the beach along the shoreline, relaxing, chatting, joking. The occasional burst of laughter, though, was quickly muted out of respect; Rabin, after all, had been assassinated only days before.

Returning to the room after one quick break, tea in hands, Palestinians were chatting with Israelis, Americans laughing with Palestinians, Israelis and Americans grabbing pens to brainstorm—our *Sesame Street* family was bonding. And it gave me an idea: Pulling the room to a focus, I said,

"We should create short films about major religious celebrations and holidays. You know, films that show how we are all connected through social and cultural traditions and cultural events in the Jewish, Christian, and Muslim calendars."

The nods from the Palestinian team froze in the deafening silence that came from the American camp.

Lewis, who was wearing his kippa, objected: "*Sesame Street* in the U.S. stays completely away from religion because of its sensitivity, and I know some of the left-of-center Israelis are really uncomfortable with focusing on it in this production particularly -- they want to avoid politicizing it."

"But my idea isn't theologically driven," I explained, "it wouldn't show bias to one religion or another. I just think it would expose Palestinian children to other peoples' cultures and traditions in religious celebrations. Think fasting: Ramadan for Muslims, Yom Kippur for Jews, and Lent for Christians. Each religion has its own cultural traditions connected with fasting holidays. And what about lights festivals that appear across all the world's major religions: the Christian Christmas tree, the Jewish Menorah, the Muslim Lantern." The Palestinians and a few of the Israelis felt on board, so I pushed on: "Our joint efforts should not just be about teaching letters and numbers. By highlighting the importance of light in our cultures, we could reflect philosophically on the importance of fighting forces of darkness, whether they be radicalism or religious intolerance from all sides."

A few nods met my rant, and Lewis began to understand that the Middle East *Sesame Streets* could not just clone their older American sibling. My idea was accepted, but there was some air of reluctance from the Americans, and I was worried about losing the good working atmosphere we had created.

Keen to keep the camaraderie alive, I tried to move our discussion to the curriculum document that we needed to get started on by the end of our time on the shores of the Sea of Galilee. The Tiberias meeting was, after all, our big introduction to *Sesame Street* and how to create the pivotal curriculum document, which the creative talent, writers, and producers would refer to throughout the production, from episode to episode.

Reaching for one of the baklawa in the middle of the table, I said, "So, this curriculum document. What do we need to know? What do we need to do?"

Lewis pulled a thick binder in front of him and banged his hand down on it. Looking up, he smiled: "Here it is. *Sesame Street*, the guidebook. Charlotte Cole, here, heads up our curriculum team and can take you through the whole thing. It looks like an epic piece of work, but when you approach it step by step, you'll be surprised how naturally it comes together."

We had already settled on our Head of Curriculum, so I looked over to her, along the table. Dr. Cairo Arafat, an American—Palestinian child psychologist and educator, would have a lead role in composing the curriculum document, drawing on her vast knowledge of Palestinian child psychology as well as preschool education. "We're counting on you, Cairo," I said, "You know this stuff, and you know how Palestinian children are going to respond."

"But," Charlotte shook her head, "it can't all be on Cairo. This must be a concerted effort: Educators, writers, creative talent, producers, everyone needs to be involved over the next few months. For this to be an effective document, we need first to agree on the topics you want to approach, then how you'll approach it, and finally get those agreed approaches down on paper in a way that everyone across the production team is going to understand. Our aim here is to bring together education, both academic and social, and lay out how the production will deal with each topic."

Cairo would be working with non-governmental organizations interested in education, like Save the Children, with the council of Palestinian private schools, and with the United Nations Relief and Works Agency for Palestinian Refugees (UNWRA), which has hundreds of schools in Gaza and the West Bank. She would also meet with people from the Ministry of Education, but not the ministry itself because, in the early days, it had not given approval for the project. So, although she would not be alone, we were certainly relying on her to make the best use of her knowledge and contacts, and we would support her in any way we could.

Charlotte went on to detail how each element in the thick binder is numbered, so when writers work on a script that needs a specific message, as each episode, segment, or animation must refer to the guidelines in the curriculum document to get that message right. As an example, she told us about the team who co-produced the Egyptian *Sesame Street* series, *Alam Simsim*, in colloquial Egyptian Arabic. They felt girls' literacy was important, so when they wrote the curriculum document that was one of the goals, a priority, which they broke down into line items or subsections, such as encouraging girls not to drop out of school, to plan and think of their career and so on.

"When the producer asks for a thirty-second animation that addresses Goal One, for example, the writers check the curriculum document for guidance. Sometimes the writers just come up with an idea first and search the curriculum document for a goal it fits. You see, you can't submit a *Sesame Street* script idea for approval without identifying a goal.

"Sometimes you have two goals, maybe language and size, or language and understanding 'the other', or respecting and tolerating people of different cultures, so all those goals should be listed on the front of the script.

"So if Khalil [Abu Arafeh, our head writer], or any of the other writers, is doing something on, say, 'big' and 'small', he or she would note on the front of the script the number of the section in the curriculum document that corresponds with teaching children to differentiate between 'big' and 'small.' This way, you can audit how focused you are on certain issues, and how you might have let others slip. It also means everyone is singing from the same hymn sheet, with the message staying consistent. By keeping the curriculum document front and center during pre-production, you'll end up with *Sesame Street* segments that are both educational and entertaining. Because every single segment in *Sesame Street* has to be fun, funny, and enjoyable at the same time as addressing at least one of the goals, and that's what makes it such an exciting challenge."

Seeing our bemused faces, Lewis leaped in:

"For much of the educational stuff—counting, the alphabet, that kind of thing," he added, "you have access to the international *Sesame Street* library, so you can use material off the shelf or tweak it to suit Palestinian children. Contractually, you should acquire and use at least fifty percent of the video footage you need for the series from the Children's Television Workshop library, anyway, but you'll also find production much easier if you do make use of the resource."

For much of the third day, Charlotte talked us through some examples of the educational videos, showing us the connection between the curriculum document and creative elements until we really started to get a feel for the process.

Slowly but surely, we got the hang of it. We did a lot of work on the alphabet. Most children in the Arab world today can sing the 'abc' song in English, but we have nothing like it in Arabic, no unifying song that helps children learn *abjadia*, the Arabic alphabet. So we brainstormed possible animations in which the Muppets do the alphabet. We discussed ways to introduce vocabulary and letters.

"But with preschoolers," Cairo pointed out, "we don't want to go too much into the pedagogical part because they won't get it. I'll take these ideas to my contacts and see what their opinions are. Great to have something to work with, though!

"At the heart of what we're doing here is for children to enjoy education, love it, be interested in it, and identify with it. What we want is for children, when they're with their parents in a car, to say 'Oh, look, Mama, it says 'souq,' or whatever, so the parents are proud and say 'Bravo, good job.' In other words, vocabulary and literacy are very important, but we don't want to get into grammar or poetry and literature."

As we got into the afternoon, we decided to take a break, having watched footage and discussed how to adapt it to suit the production, for several hours. We drifted outside, again, stretching, smoking, or making calls home, and a handful of us headed off for a stroll along the shoreline. We chatted about all we had learned: Where preschoolers were academically, and what they needed to learn; how they were likely to react to our program, and how we should reach them. We laughed as we discussed the simple jokes and the Muppet slapstick which accompanied many of the standard sketches.

Where handshaking had started our three-day workshop, we parted as a *Sesame Street* family. Filled with motivating ideas, we swapped home numbers, and went our separate ways.

Back in Jerusalem, our job next was to assemble our creative teams, search for appropriate writers, find and train the puppeteers, and get *Sesame Street* underway.

5 Pre-Production Underway

AFTER THE CURRICULUM MEETING, back in our hometowns, the political fallout of Rabin's assassination firmly placed Palestinians and their supporters in the most negative headspace they had ever been in. Even the glimmer of hope raised by the unprecedented popularity in acting Prime Minister Shimon Peres's efforts for peace was shattered by Hamas suicide bombings inside Israel. The wave of support in Israel dissipated, and the peace talks slowed down to a stutter.

Our shot at peace crumbled further by Shimon Peres's irresponsible attacks against Lebanese and Palestinians in South Lebanon. The Grapes of Wrath operation wreaked death and destruction: In one bombing, more than eighty Palestinian and Lebanese families sheltered in a UN compound in the village of Cana were killed by an air-to-land rocket fired from an Israeli fighter jet. Peres thought the war would improve his standings. The opposite happened.

The 1996 Israeli election was the first and only time Israelis voted directly for a prime minister even though the Israeli system is parliamentary. Widespread empty-ballot protest votes reflected the anger at the action of Peres's Army felt by Palestinian citizens of Israel, particularly by those with relatives who had emigrated to Lebanon.

Shimon Peres lost the elections, which just a year earlier he would have won by a landslide majority, according to the polls. Instead, right-wing Likud leader Benjamin Netanyahu won with the tiniest of majorities. Many analysts say that had the Palestinians of Galilee cast their votes for Peres instead of voting with blank cards, they might have prevented Netanyahu from taking power. The Rabin assassination had accomplished its goal of preventing the possibilities of peace. As television producers, our naïve ideas that our jobs could contribute to peace had just become near impossible.

Still, that was what we had said we would do, so we dug in and got started with pulling together *Shara'a Simsim*. We had to take care of our own diplomacy and negotiations that reached beyond politics, after all.

With our experience at JFI, we knew we would not have a problem with filming and editing the short documentaries. We could also rely on Ayman's considerable animation skills, so I asked him to make a start on them. Meanwhile, George took on the huge preparations for the studio segments. He had produced and directed some dramas but nothing the size and complexity of a world-class children's program, so he set about looking for a film maker who had worked multi-camera studio productions, an area we had little knowledge of. Adding to our list of requirements, we needed someone who would not have a hard time working with the crews at the Israeli studio. George reached out to Antoine Salah, a respected Palestinian film maker who had emigrated to Australia. That Antoine had worked in Israel and knew Hebrew, I was sure, would make it much easier for him to work with the Israeli crews. We were thrilled when he accepted the role, and when George Ibrahim, an actor on a famous Israeli children's television program *Sami and Souso*, said he would be Antoine's Assistant Director. We were all set.

As Executive Producer, I got to grips with overseeing the whole operation and coordinating with the American *Sesame Street* producers. But neither George nor I had much experience or background to help us with set design, scriptwriting, or puppetry. Thankfully Lewis sent us Josh.

Josh Selig, our great, sensitive, and knowledgeable resident producer of Jewish—Catholic parentage, was there to support both sides of the co-production, but he spent most of his time with us, negotiating with the Israelis to help things run smoothly. Josh, who pretty quickly understood and worked with the situation we were living, almost single-handedly, at times, kept the project alive.

We were like sponges, taking in everything he had to share with us. Josh helped us understand how to produce *Sesame* programs in a magazine-like format: A typical episode would have three studio segments with Muppets and/or human characters, one or two live actions (documentaries from a child's point of view), then a 2D or 3D animated or stop-action clip and songs. The songs cut across all genres, so you might have Muppets or humans sing a song, or you might couple a song with animation. "It's the songs that bring about the highest audiences," explained Josh in one of our many meetings.

Because only Khalil Abu Arafeh, our head writer and well-known *Al Quds* political cartoonist, and I were residents of Jerusalem, we were the only Palestinians on our team able to travel to Tel Aviv without a permit, so we did much of our pre-production ourselves, with Josh's help, in our tiny Ramallah headquarters. On the rare occasions the Palestinians and Israeli contingents needed to work face to face in the early days, we met in the cool of the many-windowed Pasha Room at the American Colony Hotel, in East Jerusalem. The iconic hotel, where Lewis and I first met, is just around the corner from the Jerusalem Film Institute, and it is easy for Israelis from Tel Aviv to get to because it is moments from the connecting highways. It was also where Josh Selig made his home while he was with us. From the Colony, it was quick for him to flag down a shared taxi (called in Arabic *sarvice* and in Hebrew *sherut*) and whizz down one highway or another between the Palestinian and Israeli teams, to negotiate, bargain, and generally keep the production going. But while discussions with the Israelis could be challenging, they were sometimes easier than those with the Americans in New York. At times, I felt Americans (actually Lewis) appeared more protective of Israelis and their sensitivities than the Israelis themselves. Everything we suggested, they warned us off: We were told to avoid religion in our program—no light festivals, no crosses—yet the Israelis aired a Christmas segment shot in Nazareth that showed crosses and Vatican flags.

One face-to-face meeting, though, was especially memorable as a moment that saw Palestinians and Israelis find common ground to make the project work:

For many of us, English was our second language, but it was the *lingua franca* that suited the majority, so all our fairly heated discussions were made even more frustrating as we battled with language as well as ideas. Palestinians are, by nature, generally laid-back, good-humored people, and pretty good at resolving conflict. But with so many contradictory —often poorly expressed—ideas flying around in meetings, I had to resort to my diplomacy and negotiation skills more than once. But it was during one of these moments that two of our number built bridges through language.

The Palestinian and Israeli set designers were struggling to use English to resolve a set-design issue when the Israeli designer took a phone call and spoke in Hungarian. To everybody's surprise, when she hung up, our Palestinian set designer, Samih, spoke:

"*Magyarul beszélsz?*" ("You speak Hungarian?")

It turned out that the Israeli designer was a Hungarian émigré, and Samih had studied design in Hungary. Within minutes, the frostiness between them evaporated, and the pair who had such a hard time communicating in English were in deep discussion in a language they felt completely comfortable with—even if the rest of us did not have a clue what they were saying. They went from being the least talkative at the table to one of the most productive elements of the team, thanks to Hungarian.

Happy that the set design was in good hands, George and I could turn our attention to one of the areas that were less familiar to us: scriptwriting. We knew we would have to tackle the controversial crossover segments, which would feature Palestinian and Israeli Muppets appearing on screen at the same time, but we pushed them for as long as possible—we knew they would not be straightforward, and we had enough on our plate with the Palestinian episodes.

Khalil Abu Arafeh was our extremely talented head writer, well-known for his political cartoons in *Al Quds* newspaper, where I'd met him. Despite having a brother close to the Islamists, Khalil is a totally secular leftist and remarkably creative and progressive. He has a great knowledge of differing mindsets and considerable experience in reaching groups that are often ignored, but even he found writing twenty episodes that would appeal to both Palestinian girls and boys challenging.

Appealing to girls, it turned out, was relatively easy, but appealing to boys was not because, especially at the time, the genders had very different life experiences. Living in a country where celebrities were political and writing for a program that should not reflect on politics, we struggled to find positive role models for a generation of boys that were becoming increasingly rebellious.

To help Khalil, we brought in a very talented scriptwriter, a very special young person who helped focus and guide the writing. Still just a teenager, Yara Jalajel, from the nearby town of Al Bireh, had won a writing competition and become the youngest Palestinian inducted in the Palestinian Writers' Union; her work impressed us all. She had been dabbling in all kinds of prose, so when people first saw her work, they thought that she signed her name to work done by others. Once convinced she was the author of the literature she published, local papers started running her short stories, and, soon, she was asked to join the prestigious Palestinian Writer's Association. When we first met her, she immediately impressed us with her talent, her forthrightness, and her ability to understand our task of creating scripts for *Shara'a Simsim*. Before agreeing to work with us, this incredible young woman wanted to relate to us what she thought of the only Arabic version of *Sesame Street* that had been shown on TV. *Iftah Ya Simsim*, a co-production between Sesame New York and a consortium of Arab Gulf countries, had been running *ad nauseam* on Arab TV stations since its creation in the 1980s.

"*Iftah Ya Simsim* talks down to children," she said to me with the confidence of an expert. "I have watched the program so many times that I can recall all of it for you, but I was always unhappy with the way they patronized us, as if we were stupid." Her understanding of four- to seven-year-olds' psyche was priceless.

"You're right," I said. "We want our program coming to Palestinian children with a genuine child's point of view."

What I did not say to Yara was that our New York partners and our team had similar thoughts about the program filmed in Kuwait (whose Muppets were taken back to Iraq after Saddam Hussein invaded). In reviewing some of the clips of the production, we had often laughed at the way children were dressed in their best outfits as they were filmed playing around. I remember Dr. Cairo Arafat, our content advisor, chuckling at how the little girls slid down slides wearing dresses rather than more comfortable pants.

When *Iftah Ya Simsim* was introduced, Josh and Lewis said that Sesame New York was not very pleased with the product, and that one day they hoped to revisit it with a totally new approach. (In fact, in the summer of 2011, Cairo and I participated in a workshop in Riyad,

Saudi Arabia preparing for a relaunch of *Iftah Ya Simsim* which first aired in the fall of 2015).

Yara was happy with our answers and our reassurance that our approach would be child-centered and child-friendly. I told her point blank that we expected her to reflect the children's point of view.

"I hereby appoint you Children's Ambassador to *Shara'a Simsim*," I said to her. "Your assignment is to ensure that none of the scripts talk down to our kids."

The international success of the program did not seem to faze Yara, and her ability to pull together the adults' ideas and package them for young children was truly extraordinary, helping us make great strides into the script writing, even early on. Yara used a seemingly endless source of creative ideas to develop scripts that, to this day, are held up by Sesame Street Workshop as an example of how it should be done.

Confident in their abilities, we left the writers to thrash out their early ideas and started thinking about casting our Muppeteers and adult human characters. The key, though, was the Muppeteers. While Antoine the director made his way from Australia to Jerusalem, we put a wide call out to find the right people to carry the heavy load of being the main Muppet performers on *Shara'a Simsim*. Because we were looking for Muppeteers to operate Hanin, a four-year-old female monster, and Karim, a six-year-old male rooster, we assumed we would be looking for a female and a male actor.

The Sesame Workshop organized a three-week training session for prospective actors to learn to manipulate the Muppets while acting in character. All we needed to do was arrange a large, empty room with a big mirror. So, before the trainer from the Jim Henson group came from London to work with our team of hopefuls, we rented a large dance studio in Jerusalem. Auditions started as soon as Antoine touched down, and the casting of the show was underway.

Nearly a hundred actors responded to our ads and calls, but after sifting through them, Antoine and George focused on three leading ones, Rajai Sandouka and Fadi Alghoul, who were competing to become Karim, and a female actor, who seemed to think she had the role of Hanin sewn up. In training, Fadi's talent with Muppets was immediately evident, and Rajai drew on his acting experience to create convincing characters artistic, but, quietly, the directors were not sure about the female actor.

Watching them during the three weeks of training and rehearsals, I saw the need for the mirror—with it the actors in various uncomfortable positions could see how they and their puppet would appear on screen and make their moves accordingly. The mirror also forced the actors to think counter intuitively: If they wanted the Muppet to move to the right of the screen, they needed to move physically to the left.

The trainer showed the actors how to use their right hand to manipulate the puppet then move four fingers up and down while their thumb was steady to make it talk. The first exercise appeared very simple: counting and saying the alphabet. The key was to move their fingers in sync with the words. So *wahad* (one) used two movements with the fingers to replicate the word's two syllables: 'wa' and 'had.' With three syllables, *arba'a* (four) used three movements: 'ar,' 'ba,' and 'ah.' Sneaking in to the rehearsals, I tried a bit of puppeteering. It seemed easy when I was watching, but making the Muppet lip-sync a complete sentence rather than just one word is quite a skill.

In one of the breaks, Fadi picked up Hanin's stand-in puppet and began improvising with his voice while controlling her. He had to make his voice quite shrill to imitate a four-year-old girl, but it seemed to work. Antoine and the Jim Henson trainer spotted Fadi in action and, *voila*, we were in business. We had found Hanin, and Karim was given to Rajai Sandouka, a steady, dependable, well-known actor from Jerusalem. Antoine broke it to the less-than-inspiring female actor, that she was cut and would not be working with us. Later she would claim that she left because she was unhappy with the politics of the project.

With roles assigned, the real work began. Fadi and Rajai moved away from the basic exercises and into serious rehearsals. They learnt the intricacies of manipulating Muppets for television, a surprisingly complicated process requiring incredible coordination between hand, eye, and mouth. The Muppeteers move the Muppet while remaining hidden themselves; they need to speak in character and in sync with the hand movements. And they need to do all this while laying on their back, squeezed in very tight spots, constantly checking a monitor next to them that shows what the audience will be seeing.

The whole time they were rehearsing, Fadi and Rajai used generic Muppets, called Anything Muppets, provided for training by the guys in New York. After many heated discussions tweaking colors, personalities, and attributes, all we could do was wait in anticipation for the arrival of our actual Muppets. Every now and again, we got images of them being made, so we could decide on a shape or color.

Karim, our green rooster, who represents a six-year-old Palestinian boy, and Hanin, a four-year-old, red-headed girl monster finally arrived in big boxes couriered in from the U.S. It was like Christmas morning. Opening up the boxes to see the reality of the wonderful, colorful Muppets that we had talked about, had seen drawings of, and had imagined in scripts was amazing.

Josh introduced us to Hanin first, taking her out of the box she was sitting in, using his right hand to make her mouth flutter and his left hand to operate the metal sticks that made her hands move. Suddenly Hanin became real and no longer just pieces of cloth and wires. It was an astonishing moment. It was then that it dawned on me, that it all felt very real: We really were bringing one the world's most-watched children's TV shows to Palestine.

Hanin and Karim had their own person to take care of them—a wrangler called Nancy Ishaq—whose job it was to keep them safe, clean and screen-ready. She had strict instructions to never leave the Muppets lying on the floor; they must always look alive, either on a stand or held as real entities. They are not just puppets; they are real characters that embody a belief, a dream, a hope for the future.

With most of the scripts in place thanks to Khalil and Yara, the Muppeteers learning their craft of on-camera Muppet manipulation with the Jim Hensen master and the real Hanin and Karim, we rented a large room at the Palestinian National Theater from its director and one of my friends, Jamal Gosheh, and started our search.

We had come up against some resistance to the *Sesame Street* project, which the artistic community considered rather controversial. There were those who opposed doing any project that included Israelis because they believed it would contribute to normalization of relations with our occupier, so as we moved into human-character casting, we were a little nervous about whether we would find actors willing to take on such a contentious venture.

It turned out we did not need to worry—we had plenty of applicants for the male and female adult characters. The Palestinian Theater was vibrant with excited actors looking to join us. At the end of the day of casting, Antoine and George settled on a successful Jerusalem-based actor called Hussam Abu Eisheh for the role of school music teacher, Ustaz Adel (Ustaz is 'teacher' in Arabic), who we hoped would provide a creative and artistic role model for our children. Salwa Naqara, the well-known Palestinian actress from Haifa, took the role of Im Nabil a strong, independent shop owner who is not attached or subservient to a husband or father.

Unfortunately, it proved more difficult to find younger actors, the mainstay of *Sesame Street* worldwide. We needed at least two boys and a girl character. Everyone warned us about child actors, saying that they are the hardest to find, and that they can often make or break a children's production. Antoine knew what he wanted in the child actors, and in his mind, it boiled down to a simple test of getting the children to have a chat with Hanin, to see whether they could talk naturally and convincingly to a Muppet. He obviously wanted the actor to have talent and creativity, but the most important issue for our director was that the child actor could take director's orders seriously and follow them meticulously.

During the intifada, I had become friends with the principals of the College de Frères, where my son Bishara went, and the Rosary Sisters, where Tamara and Tania, my two daughters, went. I had called the principals at both schools to ask for their help, and they welcomed our effort. I put the casting crew in touch with both, forgetting to mention they were my children's schools, and suggested that kids from the local private schools might be more self-assured and capable of shouldering such a role. The casting teams went to local—mostly private—schools and took with them a small video camera to film children at play and in conversation with Hanin.

When the auditions came, Antoine invited interested children to the theater, where they announced their first name only and acted out a few lines using a script and Antoine's directions. From behind his desk, Antoine guided each child through their audition until, by the end of the day, he awarded the role of Lila, the female child's character to a young girl called Maisa Zaidani.

As for Sami, Lila's ten-year-old brother on *Shara'a Simsim*, Antoine had, by sheer chance, chosen my son, Bishara. When Antoine told me, I laughed out loud:

"Bishara!? My Bishara? That's fantastic! What was it about him over all the others, though?" I asked.

Antoine, equally astonished, said "I didn't know he was your son! I chose him simply because—aside from his clear talent—he took my orders and executed them exactly as I asked him to."

My daughters, Tamara and Tania, had also auditioned and made it through as extras for scenes that needed more people on screen. What a day!

As I walked through the door that evening, it was hard to tell who was more excited, but I wanted him to tell me his news, so I played it cool. Bishara threw himself at me, firing off everything he had to tell me.

"Baba, Baba, I'm going to be on television, I'm going to be on *Sesame Street*. All my friends are going to be so jealous! I'm going to get money to be on TV—$1,000, Baba—a thousand! And all I had to do was talk to a Muppet. I can't believe it. Only four boys tried out when the TV people came to school today—four! I put my hand straight up when we were asked if we wanted to audition. I'm so surprised no one else wanted to do it. It's such an exciting thing to do.

"We went to the hall and a man—Antoine—introduced us to a girl Muppet called Hanin and asked me to read from a script and talk to Hanin. It was so cool! But it was strange, though, Baba; the script was all nicely typed on paper, but the words were written in Palestinian Arabic—nothing like the books we read at school. I have never seen full sentences in colloquial Palestinian Arabic written like that before."

At school, children are always given books and writing material in classical Fusha Arabic—the spoken word is rarely, if ever, seen in writing. These days you see a lot of Facebook posts written in colloquial Arabic (which drives some traditionalists nuts), but back in 1995, this seemed very odd, especially to seven-year-old Bishara. Years later, he would create an entire website using colloquial Arabic.

"You know this is the project I've been working on, Bishara?" I told my very excited son as I pulled his contract out of my bag. "Antoine, the man who auditioned you today, is the director. He didn't know you were my son before he gave you the role—he just said you were perfect for the role of Sami." Bishara beamed.

"Antoine gave me your acting contract. We need to read it through very carefully, and you need to understand what it says, then you can sign it if you agree to carry out sensibly the role and all the filming responsibilities Antoine needs you for, OK?" Bishara took signing the contract as seriously as he took his duties on set throughout his time as Sami, filming both in Ramallah and in Tel Aviv.

Day-to-day life at the Palestinian National Theater was busy, filled with director and crew working out the technical elements, Muppeteers and actors rehearsing and getting to know the ropes. I was free to give more attention to Ayman and the animation segments.

Ayman had done a fair amount of preparation while the casting was underway, so when it was time to sit down with Lewis and me, he had a lot to share.

At the time, two-dimensional animation was very costly and took vast amounts of time: Just a thirty-second animation needs storyboards for each step in the process and thousands of drawings, which are incredibly time consuming and, therefore, the most expensive part of the operation. Every second of the animation is broken into twenty-four frames, and at most you can get away with using the same image for two frames—but not more. For every second seen on TV, the animator must do at least twelve drawings, which are then colored and filmed in sequence. Watching *Tom and Jerry* cartoons on TV, viewers rarely have any idea how complicated and time consuming the operation is.

As part of our contract with New York, Sesame gave us access to their video library of animations and live-action videos curated from global *Sesame Street* franchises. We knew some elements from the library would work fine: Animations about numbers, exploring 'large' and 'small' or introducing animals or fish have no cultural identity, so we would be able to dub them effectively into Arabic and appeal to our audience, even ticking off 'awareness of the other' as a bonus.

But for culturally relevant animation and live-actions, there was no question—we would have to create our own. Drawing and producing from scratch new two-dimensional animations would be costly and not add much value even though it would improve the skills of our team. As a work-around, Lewis and Josh introduced us to a number of experts, including Jonathan Lubell, a British clay animator living in Jerusalem, to produce interesting three-dimensional animations. Jonathan had done several musical videos, including a big project with *Time Magazine* to teach English in China. But Jonathan approached the project with Ayman from a cultural point of view, and they wanted to use the technique to produce segments that can reflect Palestinian culture.

As well as the three-dimensional animations, Lewis also recommended we look into stop-action animation, which would be less expensive to produce and far more culturally relevant. The idea of stop-action animation is simple. You position a still camera to point at a small lit 'stage'—often a table or workbench. On the stage, you have any movable item you want to film. You take a shot, move the object a tiny bit and take another shot until you have many photos of the item you are filming, moving in whatever direction you want. We used this format to film small and large Arabic coffee cups on a tray, which were twirled and moved around for a simple lesson about 'large' and 'small' using a culturally relevant icon.

Jonathan and Ayman also spent a week with a large number of similar-sized pita breads and falafel balls (as well as a camera and lot of toothpicks used to keep each position in tact). They created a lovely thirty-second animation about bread and falafel with a funny ending where hot pepper surprised the pita when it was added to one of our most recognizable meals.

Over the following weeks and months, the animation team even experimented with basic graphic software to create short animations using traditional Arab tiles to illustrate various simple ideas.

In the background, I was busy working out how we would film our live-action segments. By coincidence, Hanna Elias, a Palestinian filmmaker who had done some work in Hollywood, was back in Palestine to shoot a feature film, so we approached—and quickly hired—him to take on the short documentaries. And his first documentary proved to be one of the icons of the entire program.

The writers had taken my idea of exploring Palestinian embroidery and laid out the concept for Hanna. He was to create a three-minute piece about a girl telling the story of her grandmother's Palestinian embroidery. After briefing, he seemed to know exactly what he was doing, so we left him to it. But days turned to weeks, and we still had nothing, so I had to ask him what was taking so long.

"I still haven't found the perfect girl," Hanna said. "I'm looking for a girl who has just lost her teeth, so we can represent such an important phase of childhood that is often overlooked. Simple. It won't be long, I'm sure."

He was right. Not long after, he found the girl he had been looking for and filmed with her in a Ramallah village. The three-minute video was about a Palestinian child visiting her grandmother and finding her always working on some colorful embroidery, only to discover, in the end, that Grandma was sewing a traditional Palestinian embroidery dress for her.

The segment was so colorful and authentic, and so well reflected how *Sesame Street* envisions documentaries, that the New York team often used it to showcase their work, as an example of how to meet the guidelines of filming shorts from the child's point of view, not only in Palestine but as a hold-up example of their entire international portfolio. I am told that the segment played well during talks to create a co-production between India and Afghanistan, and during a major drive to recreate *Iftah Ya Simsim*, the 1970's hugely successful first Arabic co-production, which is now being reproduced in Abu Dhabi in conjunction with the Gulf Countries Council.

But, while the toothless child and her grandmother's embroidery worked well for girls, we wanted to do something with boys as its focus; research had shown that young Palestinian males were becoming bullies in school and were rebellious at home. Cairo Arafat, the Content Director, and I talked a lot about this research. We wanted to deal with some more substantive topics and follow the New York *Sesame Street* line of having celebrities on the program. Political leaders, though, were among the only celebrities that most Palestinians knew about; I wanted something different, something in the arts or literature or maybe even sports. But we could not agree on anyone in the arts that might inspire boys. We settled on using boy scouts and sports as a way of helping direct all the energy of these boys towards a more productive goal.

In 1995, Palestine was to participate in the 1996 Atlanta Olympics. Among the Palestinian delegation was a Gazan runner, Majid Abu Maraheel, who was a member of the Palestinian Presidential guard. The national hero regularly trained on Gaza's beaches and was the perfect choice to inspire boys. Josh helped us script a great sketch between the Olympian and Hanin, the girl monster, and we were excited about it.

But the powers that be—in New York and in Tel Aviv—worried that the Palestinian and Palestinian Olympic team appearing on public TV could cause major problems. Lewis told us that the Israeli crew refused to film the segment, so we planned alternatives: filming the segment on the Tel Aviv beach using freelance camera people, or even filming the Olympian on the beach in Gaza and Hanin on blue screen. But when the day of filming arrived, and we were about to travel to Tel Aviv, violence broke out in Gaza, and the Israelis closed the Erez checkpoint connecting Gaza with Israel. In the end, we decided against the segment, sadly.

Although the project was going well, mostly, *Sesame Street* still had no TV station willing to broadcast it. As I had predicted, the newly born national Palestinian television station refused to touch the show because of its collaboration with Israel. Prayers can be answered in the strangest of ways, however: When Hatem al Husseini, the president of Al Quds University, died unexpectedly from cancer, my old schoolfriend's brother, Sari Nusseibeh, became the university's president. He approached me to set up a media studies program for the university, and I agreed—on one condition. To create an effective, all-encompassing media program, we needed a licensed TV station. He was happy to accept and endorse the station only if I brought *Sesame Street* with me. It was a done deal. He would get us a license from the Palestinian Authority, but I would have to finance and equip the station myself.

I was no stranger to fundraising after setting up and financing JFI through grants and sponsorship. I had a long list of connections I could turn to in my quest.

As a print journalist, my involvement in television was sort of accidental and was highlighted with the first Palestinian uprising in 1987. Working at the time as the editor of the English print newspaper *Al Fajr* weekly, I was regularly contacted by foreign journalists who wanted a Palestinian perspective. Many would offer me a day's pay (around one-hundred dollars) to accompany them as they visited and covered life in the Occupied Territories. It was during this period that I met Thomas Friedman of *The New York Times*, and of *The Washington*

Post Glen Frankel, Jackson Diehl, and Dan Williams, who married an Italian TV news anchor and, with her, adopted a Palestinian child. I also worked with *Los Angeles Times*' Dan Fisher and Mary Curtis, who later married *Haaretz*-reporter Ori Nir. Nir who is fluent in Arabic worked in journalism for some time, but he is now head of American Friends of Peace Now in Washington DC.

Of all the foreign media I worked with during the first days of the intifada, I was mainly with Dan Fisher from the *Los Angeles Times*. Often as Dan and I moved around, I used the Arabic term 'intifada'—which translates loosely as 'uprising' or 'resistance'—so when I saw he had used it in his *Los Angeles Times* piece, I guessed I could take a bit of the credit for getting the word out into global media and news coverage. The word has now entered the encyclopedias and become part of the Palestinian political lexicon, so much so that when Palestinians revolted in 2000, a decade later, the press immediately named it the second intifada.

It was meeting international television reporters, though, that introduced me to the world of television. I met Chris Wallace of CBS *60 minutes*, Dan Rather of *Nightline* and worked very closely with CBS's Bob Simon, who became a close friend, and whose work I very much admired. When the Iraqis imprisoned him and his crew in 1991, his wife Francoise and I organized a letter signed by Palestinian journalists who knew Bob to vouch for his professionalism and honesty in reporting and sent it to Iraqi leader Saddam Hussein. Simon was released after forty days and returned to Baghdad to do a documentary on his capture, while Saddam was still in power.

I loved Bob Simon's television reports. Unlike any other television reporter, his words and the images created a beautiful tapestry with a skill that I believe needs to be taught to any up-and-coming television reporter. My admiration for Bob, however, did not stop me from asking him and others a simple question. "Why don't you hire Palestinian crews—especially when working in the Occupied Territories?"

It is true that an Israeli cameraman working for CBS captured damning video of soldiers carrying out Israeli defense minister Yitzhak Rabin's orders in "breaking the bones of Palestinian stone throwers," but that video aside, it was strange to have Israelis, who by law have to do one-month Army reserve duty a year, filming Palestinian protestors.

"It's crazy," I pointed out to Bob, "Israeli cameramen shoot us with cameras 11 months a year, and for one month they shoot us with guns."

Bob was very frank with me: "Give me a good cameraperson or sound person, and I would hire them immediately—I don't care where they're from." And it was his challenge that pointed me down a new path in my media career in television.

A few friends and I created a television production company called Al Quds Television Productions (ATP) and were approached by an Israeli rebel, Ilan Ziv, during the first intifada. Ilan had fled to the U.S. from Israel to avoid serving in an occupying army and now he wanted to bring the Palestinian narrative to the world's attention, working with me to film the intifada. He suggested we co-produce a documentary about the intifada. We liked the idea, but we did not have trained filmmakers and knew how difficult it was for television crews to enter many of the Palestinian cities. As we talked, we came up with an idea: We would make a homegrown documentary, later named *Palestinian Diaries*, authentically chronicling life under occupation, using local film makers who we would train and equip with small Super VHS cameras—the best available at the time—and who we could meet regularly to help improve their skills.

To support them, Ilan and I worked together to raise funds. Ilan secured some funds from Britain's Channel 4 and Holland's IKON TV. We needed money for training, so we contacted the Ford Foundation who reluctantly agreed to give us a $20,000 grant, despite us being a for-profit company, which made the paperwork for the grant quite cumbersome because the foundation usually just supports not-for-profits. We had to make it clear that the grant would only be used for the training part of the production. It was as Ilan and I were working through the grant papers that Ilan put down his pen:

"Why don't you create a not-for-profit organization? You'd have much better access to training grants that way."

Of course! It made perfect sense. And as we talked that afternoon on the fourth floor of the Nuzha building outside the ATP offices, we thrashed out the founding ideas for setting up the Jerusalem Film Institute (JFI). Thanks to *Palestinian Diaries* and my work supporting international TV crews, I had become familiar with the needs of television news reporting and began learning about making documentary films. But for the Jerusalem Film Institute, I wanted to work with a Palestinian filmmaker and producer, someone more into film than television, so we could merge the formats.

George Khleifi, a well-known, well-respected Palestinian filmmaker joined me, and together we organized film nights, held a film festival and began running film and animation workshops. I traveled to the States to visit David Hoffman, the president of Internews, who committed the foundation's financial support and introduced me to the Open Society Institute, which donated $100,000 to our project. On another U.S. trip, I managed to secure further core funding to our institute from the Ford Foundation.

We also had held many seminars discussing the need to be prepared for a Palestinian TV station. In early 1991, at our Palestinian Film Festival, I warned a group of colleagues and fellow artists that if we did not start preparing immediately, we would one day find ourselves holding a license for a television station but have no one to work in it because we lacked training.

But here I was, in 1996, with a trained crew, actors and a world-class program—ready to get a new station underway. I would get the funding for the station, no question.

56　*Sesame Street*, Palestine

Poster of the first season using the Arabic alphabet.

Daoud Kuttab Meeting with King Abdullah II at Princeton University 2007.
Personal archive.

Daoud Kuttab and his wife Salam Madanat meeting the King.
Personal archive

58 Sesame Street, Palestine

Daoud and Salam Kuttab with Hollywood actor Richard Gere during his visit to Palestine and Jordan in 2003. Personal archive.

Shara'a Simsim season three crew with Palestinian Prime Minister Salam Fayyad, and Sesame CEO Gary Knell and Lewis Bernstein.

Photos 59

Script writing workshop for season three with Nada Al Yassir. Personal archive.

Howard Sumka, USAID West Bank and Gaza director speaking at the launch of season four in Bethlehem. Photo courtesy of Sesame Palestine.

To the right of Palestinian Minister of Education Lamis Alami, Sesame CEO Mel Mind and Lewis Bernstein in January 2013. Daoud to her left.
Daoud Kuttab private collection.

Layla Sayegh (in red) Palestine Sesame project manger with the CEO of the Palestinian Jawwal company Ammar Aker (between Lewis and Mel Ming).
Private archive.

To the right of Palestinian Minister of Education Lamis Alami, Sesame CEO Mel Mind and Lewis Bernstein in January 2013. Cairo Arafat to her left. Daoud Kuttab private collection.

From far right of the muppets Cairo Arafat, Layla Sayegh, Puppet Haneen, Howard Sumka, Official of the Palestinian government, Puppet Kareem, Daoud Kuttab and a ministry of education official. Photo courtesy of Palestine Sesame team.

62 ◼ *Sesame Street*, Palestine

Full size muppets putting on a show for Palestinian children in Bethlehem. photo courtesy of Palestine Sesame team

Palestinian children attending live show of Shara'a Simsim in Bethlehem wearing t-shirts from the project. photo courtesy of Palestine Sesame

6 Israelis Visit with an M16

My fundraising tour secured enough to create and equip our TV station. We had wanted to headquarter it in Jerusalem, but the Israeli government did not allow it, so we settled, instead, for a great location at Al Quds University in Ramallah, a twenty-minute drive from Jerusalem (on a good day). Being on campus also made it easier for me to develop the media program Sari Nusseibeh had asked for.

The team had made great strides in pre-production while I was in the States, and, although we now had what was to become the smallest sound stage in the world to record *Sesame Street*, our month filming in Tel Aviv was fast approaching. We needed to make arrangements and finalize how that month was going to work: The set crew had questions about dimensions and transport logistics, many of the crew needed to have visas and travel documents sorted, and there was any number of bits and pieces we had to work through.

While we could have met at the American Colony again, we wanted to show our Israeli counterparts how well things were going on our side of the production. Over months of meetings, a bond had formed between both teams, so I thought it would be a positive step to invite the Israelis to our offices.

Proud of all we had achieved, I asked Josh to make the invitation when he was next in Tel Aviv, but when he walked back into my office, I knew something was wrong.

"They won't come," he said. "They say they can't."

A flash of anger flooded me—once again, we were being snubbed. They just could not be bothered to go out of their way to make this happen. I spun my chair away from Josh, flushed on the other side of my desk, and clasped my fingers together, taking a moment to calm down by looking out over the courtyard at Al Quds. I took a few deep breaths and a nervous glance from Josh, which I smiled at, and picked up the phone. I asked for Dolly Wolbrum—the Executive Producer on the Israeli *Sesame Street*—figuring a conversation from one executive producer to the other would have more chance of success.

If nothing else, having a Palestinian push for meetings (something the Israelis were always in favor of)—albeit on our grounds—might embarrass them into coming. She was polite but firm as she explained she had no power to make the trip possible—this was how it was. As Israeli civil servants of a public TV station, they needed official approval from a government agency to travel into what is called Area A, an area totally under the control of the Palestinian security.

The Israeli—Palestinian agreement, the 1993 Oslo Accords, had divided the West Bank into three areas: Area A, the populated urban city boundaries, and from which the Israeli Army withdrew in the initial phase, leaving the Palestinian Authority with administrative as well as lightly-equipped police control. Area C included all the settlement areas and their surroundings; the Jordan Valley and all east Jerusalem were considered under full Israeli administrative and security control. What remained was termed Area B—the outlying areas just beyond the city limits—and fell under Israeli security control but Palestinian administrative control; in other words, in Area B, the Palestinians pick up the garbage, but the Israelis patrol the streets.

"Ramallah is in Area A. We've been officially barred from coming because our insurance won't cover it," said Dolly.

I laughed—such a simple problem could easily be solved—"Why don't you simply increase the insurance fee to cover your team's visit to Ramallah?'

But apparently it was not that simple.

Here we were taking a huge political chance on a joint children's program that our team was filming entirely in Tel Aviv, with both nation's characters appearing on the same screen, and the humans working on the program were not be able to visit us. It was simply unacceptable, but even Josh's smooth talking could not change the situation.

Still keen to host the Israelis, I worked up a solution. A compromise. Instead of traveling to Ramallah, where the bulk of our talent lives and where my university office, our Media Institute, and our TV station are, the Israeli team could visit the Star2000 studios in Al-Ram in Area B, i.e. under Israeli security control, and I could arrange for the Ramallah-based talent to make the short trip out from Ramallah.

The compromise meant the Israelis would not get to see our Institute of Modern Media, nor Al Quds Educational TV station, two institutions we were extremely proud of. For us, though, it was not about showcasing equipment, which the Israelis surely had, but the fact that we were laying the groundwork for our state culturally and educationally, and not just focusing on politics and the ongoing security issues.

Star2000, a purely Palestinian company, was handling day-to-day production out of a converted three-bedroom apartment half way between Ramallah and Jerusalem, in Al-Ram, just three minutes from my home in Qalandia. With simple workstations and a couple of desktop computers, we had all we needed. Ever the businessman pushing for sales, Raed Andoni, the company's owner, had stuck on the wall a poster of a large video-editing machine to greet visitors. Our reception area had a high table and a secretary sitting behind it, answering the company's one phone, feeding the fax, and occasionally preparing coffee when we had a big group.

Raed and I arrived at the same time, so we grabbed our morning coffee and had a chat with producer George, head writer Khalil, and some of the staffers who were also topping up on caffeine on what felt like an historic day: The Israelis were coming to us.

I figured that they were most likely going to arrive on time, unlike a typical Arab visitor who is routinely ten to twenty minutes late, a stereotype we wanted to break using our ever-punctual rooster, Karim.

Comically, in fact, they were a little late.

Knowing she would be on waitressing duty as well, the secretary clattered around, stocking up the tea and Nescafe; under a Sony promotional poster, she prepared the *meramia* sage she had brought from home in case our guests were interested in trying our local herbal tea.

While waiting to get the call that the Israelis were close, Raed and I made sure we were on the same page with what we needed to talk about in the joint meeting:

"Sets, studio issues and permits," Raed said, clearly ahead of the game as usual.

"I really want this to be a success," I said. "Let's focus on creating a collegial atmosphere. The *meramia* is a great idea. Maybe we can show the Israelis some of our animation ideas as well. Is the falafel stop-action edited?'

Ayman and Jonathan Lubell had designed and filmed, over two full days, the twenty-second animation of a talking pita bread, which ends when the pita asks for hot sauce, finds it too hot and rushes off leaving a trail of cucumber and tomato behind it. Ayman had used over thirty pita loaves, as each tiny movement of the talking pita had to be shot separately. With so many moves to film a few seconds of animation, Raed said of the course the editing was not finished, but we could show them the embroidery short documentary, a favorite of mine. This was the video I wanted them to see, and I told Raed to queue it up to be ready when the Israeli team arrived.

The call came telling us the Israelis were near. Raed went into his office to finish up some business before the day started, while the others went to check the makeshift conference room was set up properly, and I headed out into the growing heat to greet Dolly, her director, head writer, and a few of the other staffers who had been willing to take 'the risk' and come to Palestine in a minibus to work on the project.

* * *

WE SHOOK HANDS WARMLY, and I escorted our guests into the office, where I introduced them to Raed, George and Khalil. Our set designer, Samih, was on hand for this meeting to discuss issues of size, height, and modes of transporting the sets to Tel Aviv.

"Did you have any problems getting here?" I asked.

"No, it was an easy drive. It's a very pretty area, isn't it?"

"Very! Were there any checkpoints?"

Of course, the Israelis had no problems with checkpoints, but they are such a typical part of the Palestinian day that it was a natural question to ask our guests.

Raed had to take a call, while the rest of us strolled together into the meeting room, down the hall from reception, and as we settled the receptionist offered drinks:

"We have tea or Nescafe or our local *meramia*, if anyone wants to try it," she said in English.

There was an ice-breaking giggle around the room as everyone ordered a Nescafe, until finally one of the Israelis said he would give the *meramia* a go. A stifled cheer ushered the receptionist out of the room. I introduced the embroidery short standing in front of another of Raed's promotional posters: an oversize one of a twenty-four-channel mixer.

From behind our pushed-together desks, the Israelis applauded at the end of the embroidery short. The painstakingly chosen toothless six-year-old girl narrating her visit to her grandmother's house gave us a glimpse into her world as she watched her grandmother embroider. Her lack of teeth gave the little girl the fantastically human, real edge Hanna had wanted to fill his vision. Excited chatter filled the room and compliments flew about the choice of toothless girl, the camera angles, and the narrating skill of the child.

On a high, most of us started discussing the set design and logistics of getting it to Tel Aviv. Khalil, however, looked intently at one of the Israeli team, apparently listening—but the Palestinian team knew what he was up to. His pencil scratched across the pad; first a pair of eyes appeared, staring out from the page, then the face took shape. Some quick strokes to emphasize the hair and the rest of the body, and Khalil signed and dated it, then flicked to an empty page. His love of doodling had caused many chuckles through the months of work and meetings in our now–close-knit group, and maybe he hoped to build a bridge with the Israelis in the same way.

He had just started his next sketch when a yell cut through the discussions; eyes flicked around the table but we stayed put. Raed was screaming at someone. I had no idea why he would be angry, but, knowing Raed, I figured it must be important; Raed is not always a very warm person, especially at work, where he is a no-nonsense manager. But the shouting did not stop: The yells we were hearing were not the kind between a manager and a tardy staff member, or worker who had made a costly mistake. It had the passion that reflected the deep anger, and, yes, the hatred that people in our region have.

"...not obliged..." we heard, "...in our own office..."

"I won't take this..." screamed Raed's voice, livid and loud.

In a flash of adrenalin, I dropped my pen and, an Israeli staffer and Dolly behind me, led the charge towards the lobby, nervous about what I might be running into.

We arrived to see the back of Raed's head and the receptionist's very large eyes, which darted from Raed, to us and then to an Israeli security man, dressed in a dark blue safari-type shirt, standing next to the door of the little room.

As the security man turned towards our group, I saw it: an M16 gun. He clearly had another weapon stashed at his side as well. The Israelis, who created the much smaller UZI gun, prefer the American semi-automatic, which is physically both imposing and unmistakable. It is practically impossible to miss the M16, and Raed clearly had not.

Raed was skinnier but taller than the bulky Israeli security man. Probably in his mid-thirties, the Israeli's upper body was one solid block of intimidating muscle. His face, however, told a different story. Flustered by being shouted at in an office with a delegation taking steps to peace, the Israeli's bad English worsened, making his attempts to say he was just doing his job even harder to accept. Raed had a clear advantage.

Raed turned to us and ranted:

"What is this? They don't trust having their people in an office with us without a security guy armed with an assault rifle? We must deal with this indignity at checkpoints, but now it's in my own office? I saw plenty of guns when I was in prison, I don't need to see guns here.

"We begged them to come to this office. How dare he be here—he doesn't trust us. They don't trust us. Get him out! Get out! Get out!"

Raed's fury was overwhelming and was very capable of sabotaging the meeting, destroying the collegial spirit we had worked so hard to create and preserve. Everyone was dumbfounded. Stunned silence reigned.

Sure, the scene was disturbing, but, in a crazy way, also liberating. The Alice in Wonderland Show was over. We did not need to walk on eggshells anymore. That M16 dragged us back to the political reality of a military occupation and an angry Palestinian population, unwilling to quit or to accept being ruled without putting up a fight—even a verbal one.

Words in Hebrew started to fly. Dolly and her team flustered through their embarrassment: This was clearly the last thing that they wanted, too. They knew they were safe with us, and the hurried hand gestures that animated the Hebrew told us they understood they needed to act, and quickly.

Dolly must have convinced the security guard that his presence was not making her and the other Israelis safe; on the contrary, his presence had created a potentially dangerous situation. They must have instructed him to stay on guard outside, preferably in the van, and to stay as inconspicuous as possible.

While it never occurred to me then, with hindsight, I think that following his charges into the office was more for the guard's own sense of security: Being inside a building must surely have felt less vulnerable than sitting alone, outside, in a territory where he was unwelcome. Had he asked, had he left his ugly bloody killing machine outside, we would have made him tea and gladly accommodated him.

That said, he could hardly leave an unattended M16 in a minivan as he sipped tea in a television studio. His predicament illustrated the whole political problem: The military and its occupation had become not only a huge burden on us but also a burden on Israel and Israelis.

The occupation was no longer an asset.

With the security guard and his M16 out of the office, we returned to the meeting room and tried to reconnect, to rekindle the atmosphere we had achieved before the incident. With a smile on her face, the receptionist pushed open the door with the front edge of the drinks' tray. As we each enjoyed the security that comes from a hot drink, and the social inspiration it offers, we started chatting. We applauded the Israeli who had braved the *meramia* and teased those that had not, and as the atmosphere thawed, discussion about set dimensions, logistics, and travel administration for the month in Tel Aviv got underway.

At the end of the day, Khalil handed a signed and dated caricature to Dolly, the emotion of the historic day seemed to lift for her before a gaggle gathered around her:

"Oh, it looks so much like you," said Josh

Sesame Street, Palestine

"I look so stressed ... but I guess that's no big surprise!" said Dolly. Our day hosting the Israelis had been a success—M16s aside—and there was an excitement about the coming month of filming in Tel Aviv.

7 Smuggling and Filming in Tel Aviv

WITH FUNDING IN PLACE, we started work on our own studios on the fourth floor of a building that used to be the Hilton hotel in Ramallah. What would become the Institute of Modern Media at Al Quds University was underway, but day-to-day meetings, scriptwriting and set planning for *Shara'a Simsim* still happened in Al-Ram at Star2000.

The studios were far from ready, though, and what later would be the smallest sound studio in the world to produce *Sesame Street* needed a lot of work before it was useable. So, we needed to find somewhere to do the filming. Palestine TV had already said they wanted nothing to do with the project and did not have studios anyway, so that was not an option. Most other production companies just had small news studios, which could never accommodate something on *Sesame Street* scale. Quite simply, we did not have studios big enough to contain our set.

Our creative team had written scripts that required a huge set with a courtyard, a sweet shop, houses on the side, a backdrop of arid hills and olive trees, a meeting place around a water spring, and the homes of our human characters: Ustaz Adel, the musical school teacher, and Im Nabil. We needed a large studio, and the only option we had was what the Israel Executive Director, Dolly Wolbrum, offered us. We had no choice but to transport everything we needed for filming—set, cast, Muppeteers and crew—to Tel Aviv's Educational Television in Ramat Aviv, an upscale Tel Aviv suburb.

To save money and time and to benefit local business, our Hungarian-speaking set designers suggested we build the set in Ramallah and transport it to Tel Aviv for filming. With the dimensions of the Tel Aviv studio constantly in mind, the designers took their time to create a set that would make most of the space available to them. Throughout the planning process, they needed to consider not just how the set would look on screen, but how the actors would interact with it, and, more importantly perhaps, how the Muppeteers would perform their roles while on their back, crawling about, or sitting cooped up in a tiny space, whatever they had to do so the Muppet could be seen on camera and the Muppeteers stayed invisible. They fashioned a modular set and stored each piece as they finished it in a big warehouse in Ramallah's industrial zone, ready for transport and reconnection once in the studio.

Moving the massive sets required we rent a truck from East Jerusalem, a Palestinian city that the Israelis had unilaterally annexed to Israel. Because of East Jerusalem's annexation, all Jerusalemites have permanent residency in Israel, so their vehicles (including trucks) have Israeli license plates, which makes travel across checkpoints considerably easier than with plates from the Occupied Territories. Without them, the hour drive to Tel Aviv in a truck filled with Palestinian carpentry and tools would have taken far longer, no matter how many permits, letters, and phone calls we made.

While getting the massive set to Israel was a challenge, and arranging travel permits and work papers for the Palestinian cast and crew for a month was time consuming and frustrating, it was only when we tried to make arrangements for our main Muppeteer, Fadi Alghoul that things really got tricky. The Israeli Army simply refused him a permit. Fadi's parents were from Gaza, but he was born abroad and had only moved to Palestine when his father, a cadre with the PLO, had been allowed to return shortly after the signing of the Oslo Accords in 1993. Since his family was registered in Gaza, the process of getting a Gazan living in Ramallah permission to go to Tel Aviv proved impossible. The only answer was to smuggle him in.

As a Jerusalemite and an American citizen, my relative freedom to move between Israel and the Occupied Territories, as well as internationally, paid off many times throughout the project. I felt I had a duty to share the liberties my nationality offered me with those who face constant discrimination at borders and checkpoints. One of my staffers, for example, was invited to the U.S. for a three-week government-sponsored tour; however, he needed to pick up the approved visa waiting for him in Jerusalem. He had tried to get to Jordan to collect it from the U.S. embassy in Amman but was turned back by the Jordanians, who insisted he could go through Jordan only when he had a visa for the U.S.—a catch twenty-two. To save the day, I smuggled him into Jerusalem and the nearest U.S. Consulate. We chose to pass through the Pisgat Zeev checkpoint, in the largest residential neighborhood in Jerusalem, because it is so frequently used by Israeli settlers. Smuggling Palestinians across checkpoints that Israelis also pass through is easy because the soldiers cannot afford to stop every car. There is a certain art required: The driver must act with so much confidence that the young soldier staffing the checkpoint does not dare stop the car. I went through without looking at the soldiers, drove into Jerusalem on Nablus Road, and dropped the staffer off at the U.S. Consulate. An hour later, he called me—visa in hand—to pick him up and smuggle him out again.

For our month of filming in Tel Aviv, however, I realized more than ever how grateful and blessed I was for my birthright.

While work on *Sesame Street* took off, my personal life took a turn for the worse: My wife, Nuha, had been diagnosed with breast cancer, and the prognosis was not good. Every day, I drove the two-hour round trip to Tel Aviv to be with her and the children, and to make the most of the time we had left together.

As I was driving daily to Tel Aviv, I said I would be able to get Fadi to Tel Aviv. Since my car is from Jerusalem and technically Israeli, and as, at the time, no walls existed, we could slip easily across the green line separating the West Bank from Israel. We decided to use a range of checkpoints people are not usually stopped at—and simply avoided any of the more problematic checkpoints.

Even on our first trip, it was relatively easy to relax during the drive. I picked Fadi up from his home in Ramallah and headed for the checkpoint. As we sped through without slowing down, the permitless Fadi and I chuckled about some of the more ridiculous situations we had sneaked about in over the years. Palestinians learn early to avoid detection, to move around without others noticing. As a teen, I slinked out to see my first-ever movie in a Bethlehem cinema, despite my dad's tough restrictions. Dad preached to us that cinema was from the devil, but I wanted to join my classmates to see Sidney Poitier in *To Sir with Love*, the latest flick playing in Bethlehem. Fadi and I were amused by the fact that Sidney Poitier's character inspired and motivated underprivileged, unmotivated London kids to believe in themselves and to appreciate learning—and here we were doing the same with the *Sesame Street* message we wanted to share in Palestine, twenty-seven years later.

Once in Tel Aviv, we assumed it would be plain sailing, but we were caught off guard. Or, actually, by the guards. We were stunned to find the studios had a private Israeli guard company deployed to check every single person. Never did we think the problem would literally be on our doorstep for the entire month.

"It was, without a doubt," said Josh in an article he wrote for *The New York Times* in March 1998, "the most heavily armed television studio I had ever been to. In addition to the three guards at the gate with automatic weapons, another guard was permanently stationed outside the studio where the Palestinian team was taping. I don't know if this was standard policy or if the Palestinian puppets just looked particularly dangerous." [1]

Moving Fadi past the private security personnel at the studio entrance was far more difficult than we had expected, so we had to ask Dolly, the Israeli Executive Director, to get him in without security realizing what we were doing. She used the same bravado we used when crossing borders—confidence, it seems, is all when you are doing what you should not.

Sneaking out from home is a rite of passage most kids go through, but sneaking around to avoid security forces—especially on a project designed to forge positive relationships—is not something grown men and women should have to endure; though it is something we are quite used to doing as Palestinians—and as Israelis, I learnt in Tel Aviv—and it is a skill I needed more than once to keep production moving.

Josh wrote about that first day of filming in his *The New York Times* piece: "Once in the studio, the two teams themselves mingled cautiously and the atmosphere was not unlike a high-school dance before anyone has started dancing. Fortunately, Cathy Chilco, the vice

---

1. *Muppets Succeed Where Politicians Haven't* JOSH SELIG (NYT), March 29, 1998 *New York Times*

president of *Sesame Street* International Production, arrived and made a bold executive decision: dinner for both teams at a restaurant on the Mediterranean.

"This was the first time all the Israelis and all the Palestinians had spent an evening together and Cathy saw to it that everyone sat, more or less, Israeli-Palestinian-Israeli-Palestinian, the regional equivalent of boy-girl-boy-girl. Soon the dancing had begun. The children of the intifada, the Palestinian uprising, were toasting the children of kibutzniks. The conversations were in Arabic, Hebrew, English and (for some reason) Hungarian, and the topics were far more likely to be about puppets than politics.

"After that evening, a true spirit of friendship began to take hold in the crowded IETV studio. During breaks, the Israelis and the Palestinians had coffee together, with or without their American chaperones. People touched one another when they talked."

And Josh was right: Despite logistics problems, the month in Tel Aviv saw many barriers broken down. Both Palestinian and Israeli actors and crew gained a better understanding of each other's cultures and lifestyles, and there was a clear building of mutual respect and friendships.

We had been warned about the difficulties of working with the Israeli crews running the studio—they had a hard-nosed reputation of being aggressive and intolerant, hostile and uncooperative, but Cathy's meal out led the way in forging a positive, productive atmosphere, in which everyone genuinely appeared to get along well. Israelis who had worked with the IETV crew before asked us what we had done to get them 'behaving,' being so professional and non-aggressive. Even Israel Educational Television management could not believe how well behaved the Israeli crew was, wondering if they were being unusually cooperative because of the importance of the project and the presence of Palestinians—or the Americans.

"Who can say?" I answered. "Maybe it's George's natural charm ..." George Ibrahim, one of the few Palestinian actors famous on both sides, had his own show that he shot during meal times and coffee breaks. George, whose real name is George Habash (the same name as the famous Palestinian leader from the Popular Front for the Liberation of Palestine), had starred in an Israeli TV children's program called *Sami and Soso*, which was also directed by Antoine Salah. When George arrived on set, workers, staff, and passersby would salute him and ask him to repeat famous lines from the children's program, which most of them seemed to remember.

"… Or it might have been his *arguileh*, his water pipe!" I joked. Clearly feeling at home and every bit a celebrity at the Israeli Educational TV, George, the Assistant Director to Antoine Salah, had brought with him what I thought was prohibited in public in Israel. Maybe inspired by my smuggling in of Fadi, George had with him all the elements of a water pipe, which he would take his time assembling each day. With the glass vase filled with water and all the components in place, he piled it with hot coals—from where they came, I have no idea—and loaded in his own cherry tobacco. Then he drew heavily on the mouthpiece to get the smoke moving through the water to filter it, letting out billows of cherry aroma through the canteen in his spare moments.

He called people over, openly sharing the *arguileh* with friends and passersby. I was embarrassed by this, sure it was not allowed, but I guessed the Israelis wanted to show good will and, assuming this was part of normal Palestinian culture, chose not to intervene or ask him to remove his water pipe. Maybe they were keen to avoid a diplomatic problem, but I would have happily supported them had they asked him to stop.

If George was not the source of our success with the Israelis, it could have been related to the huge respect many had for the veteran Palestinian Director Antoine Salah, who many knew either through reputation or from working with him over the years. Antoine, who had emigrated to Australia, kept strong links with the Palestinian territories and had worked on several high-profile productions in Israel, too. On set, he ran a tight ship, and while he was not especially kind to the crew and cast, he was in control, which seemed to put everyone at ease because they knew what was expected of them.

It is also possible the agreeable working environment may just have been down to the project being so unique, with such a clear focus on helping the next generation do a better job at peace than we had. Dealing every day with forward-thinking ideas that promoted tolerance and acceptance seeped into daily life for the actors, Muppeteers, and crew of both the Israeli and Palestinian teams. Given the Palestinians' relative inexperience, our dedication, and attention to detail during work in the studio impressed even the hardened Israeli crew members. Across the divisions, friendships and some good working relationships forged.

Josh noted in his article: "No one was immune to the love fest. Even the Palestinian team's most vocal anti-Israeli member, Nancy Ishaq, who had lost a half-brother during the intifada, surprised us all one day by sporting a toy ring she had been given by an Israeli crew member and announcing: 'Look! I am engaged to a Jewish!' She had not become engaged, of course, but she had done something that for her was almost as radical. She had made her first real Israeli friend."

And love really was in the air at times. There was a bit of harmless flirtation between one of our young assistant producers—who later became director—and a young Israeli woman, but when his girlfriend back in the West Bank heard about this, she moved fast to push her parents to make the final commitment. They were married less than a year later and the Palestinian producer has become a celebrity in the Palestinian cinema world—still happily married.

With so much positivity around me, by day I was engrossed in the project and filming, with its many details, and every evening as Nancy put the Muppets to bed, I drove back to Jerusalem to spend quality time with the family. At home I was no longer the executive producer, but a dad, and husband. There was nothing I liked more than getting home to my family every evening—to spend time with Nuha, who was now very sick.

"How was your day, Daoud?"

"Pretty successful, as it turns out!" I flopped next to her on the sofa as she muted the set. "You know Fadi—Alghoul—? You know! The guy who was the right-hand Muppeteer for Karim the rooster? Well, he was practicing using Hanin—the girl monster Muppet—during the coffee break, and he had everyone in stitches … he's perfect for her! So now he's operating Hanin all on his own. Obviously, we'll have to find a new right-hand for Karim, but we couldn't give this chance up."

"Do you have the tapes from today? I'd love to see the 'new' Hanin—and see how Bishara is getting on. I'm so proud of him … and of you. Maybe I'll get to come into the studio to watch the filming soon—when I'm better."

"We have every reason to be proud of him. We'd love to show you around whenever you're ready." I loaded the VHS into the player. George Khleifi, also a family friend, gave me unedited reels from the day's filming, so I could see how things were coming along. Nuha and I snuggled in.

There was no denying it: Hanin's character came across so much better with Fadi operating her. We got a sense of the four-year-old's character causing chaos for her far more restrained 'rooster' brother, Karim, and watching Nuha laughing aloud at their antics confirmed our decision to exchange the Muppeteers.

I paused the tape and told Nuha about the next scene: "You'll love this! Bishara did great today. He was up on the wall with Hanin, and Fadi was crouching behind. Overlooking the well, they sang 'our' alphabet song together."

Nuha welled up "Like the millions of English-speaking children use to learn their alphabet? Oh, how wonderful! Do you think it'll catch on the same?"

"That's the plan."

But with the alphabet differing across the region, I doubted it would be quite so wide-reaching. Countries in the Levant (Palestine, Syria, Lebanon, and Jordan) say *aleph, ba, ta, tha*, while those in Egypt and North Africa say *aleph, ba, jim, da, ha*. There is even something of a cultural war going on between Damascus-based entertainment and Cairo-based. In fact, neither really pays much attention to children's edutainment,

I flicked the machine back on again. "Let's see! Do you think it will?"

And we watched as Bishara and Hanin enchanted us with their *aleph, ba, ta, tha* version.

My days were so filled with charging around that all too often I did not get the chance to just enjoy the fruits of my labor. Sitting with Nuha and laughing those evenings away was a large part of my reward in the early days. And having our son as the hero alongside the Muppets was certainly the icing on the cake.

8 Crossovers: Putting Israelis on a Palestinian Street

I RUBBED MY FOREHEAD. It had been another long day—fun and successful—but long. The drive from my home north of Jerusalem to the Tel Aviv Educational Television studios out on the coast took an hour on a good day. I had only been stopped for a short while at the checkpoint, but it still added time and stress to the journey.

My daughter cuddled close as we chatted about the day's filming before she drifted off. Easing myself away and tucking her under the sheet, I kissed her on the forehead and turned out the lamp next to her bed. All of this was for her—for all my children—and I took strength from those moments of calm because the next few days were going to be tough.

I closed the door behind me and, as I passed his room, checked on Bishara, who had also had a busy day on set, and I willed myself into the living room where Nuha, a shadow of the woman I married, had fallen asleep in front of the TV, a moment's escape from the reality of the cancer wrecking her body.

I helped her to bed, switched off the light, poured a tea in the kitchen then walked out to the balcony. Leaning against the railing, with the tea warming my hands, I looked out over Qalandia refugee camp. I watched the moon reflect off the twists of metal that poked towards the sky, and, behind the concrete slab walls that fractured us from Jerusalem, the lights of TV sets still flickered in a few windows. With a couple of weeks of filming in Tel Aviv already done, it would not be long before we sent *Sesame Street* into those homes—but we still needed to work out how to put Israelis and Palestinians on the *Sesame Street* screen at the same time.

Over months of preparations and meetings, our Palestinian and Israeli teams had developed the mutual support and cooperation that everyone at Children's Television Workshop in New York had been hoping for, but that cordiality had not made it on to the screen, yet. The filmed episodes were exclusively in Palestinian Arabic, and their focus was on Palestinian culture, traditions, and stereotypes.

More than anything, we wanted our children to be proud of their roots, of the rich culture they were growing up in, so if we had our way, our production would stay purely Palestinian. But in a well-meaning attempt to bring the peace process to the common Palestinian, the Americans footing the bill were pushing for ten 'crossover segments,' where Israelis and Palestinians would appear in the same scenes on screen, in the twenty-episode series. The Americans wanted us to write ten crossovers, but it was unrealistic; in no way was having Israelis and Palestinians appearing side by side for fifty percent of the production representative of the Palestinian—or Israeli—experience.

I completely support the peace process and believe that teaching tolerance and mutual respect is the way to a more secure future, but ramming concepts of peace down the throats of young children before true peace had been realized felt contrived.

Our focus needed to be on children's development, and adding the political element made it difficult to focus on the necessary basics: Three-quarters of Palestinian children never made it to preschool before starting first grade. Our teachers struggled with first-graders far more on an emotional than an educational level. Children suffered life skills problems; they lacked self-confidence and struggled with being away from their mothers.

But however unnatural the crossover segments felt, our contract had us tied in. The Americans were right: We should have started writing the crossover segments before starting production. Josh, our part-time peace negotiator and envoy from the States, had orders from the Children's Television Workshop to ensure we create the crossover segments. We had chuckled several times during pre-production as his commitment and genuine enthusiasm for the crossovers spilled over into coffee breaks, into lunch, and on the way out of the building at the end of the day; whenever he had a chance, Josh would grab one or more of us to talk about the crossovers.

A couple of days before, though, he had really started to put on the pressure: "There's only a couple of weeks filming left. You have to get the crossovers written. They have to work—there's no option to drop them."

"OK, I know! But having ten crossover segments, as the Americans want, just isn't realistic. To keep the show relevant and believable," I reasoned, "having Israelis on the Palestinian street needs to be kept to a minimum. What if we reduce them. Instead of trying to create ten, maybe we could come up with three. How do you think the Americans and Israelis would feel about that? Could you ask them for us?"

Josh rolled his eyes and managed to smile as he heaved his backpack over his shoulder and went to catch another shared taxi back to Jerusalem. From there he would go to Tel Aviv to negotiate. I felt bad for him, but he knew how best to find a happy compromise for everyone, and I had agreed with Lewis right from the start that we would only deal with New York—through Josh—and not get involved in negotiations with the Israeli side.

The following day Josh reappeared with a quiet smirk.

"Do you want the good news?"

"Just hit me with it."

Josh breathed deeply.

"They'll accept three crossovers."

"Great!" I still did not really want any crossovers, but I figured we could come up with something, mainly because we had to. We had been avoiding writing the crossovers since we were told about them in Tiberias in November 1995, but half way into our month of filming in Tel Aviv, we could not avoid them anymore. It was crunch time. On the balcony, I took a deep swig of my tea, now cold, so poured another one and headed for my computer. The blinking black line under the title 'Crossover Segment Ideas' on the screen in front of me, tormented me. Still I had nothing.

How could we possibly bring the two radically different 1996 worlds together onscreen when peace in the off-screen world had still not been implemented? Palestinians were still waiting for the Oslo Accords framework to come into effect, even though it had been established three years previously when Rabin and Arafat shook hands on the White House lawn on September 13, 1993. Negotiations were dragging, Israeli settlement activities were continuing, and Palestinian extremists, skeptical or simply afraid of peace talks, were still carrying out suicide attacks. Nothing of the Palestinian—Israeli experience, at the time, really lent itself to a children's program that preached tolerance and respect for 'the other.'

Our brief was to produce crossovers, so one or more of the Israeli Muppets, Kippi, a large purple porcupine with a heart of gold, in many ways like Big Bird, Moishe Oofnik—a bit like Oscar the Grouch—or the new one, Dafi, a purple monster, could appear on *Shara'a Simsim* with our Muppets, Karim and Hanin. The Israelis were actively writing and filming segments about the appearance of our Muppets on *Rehov Sumsum* (*Sesame Street* in Hebrew), but that did not concern me: My focus was on what Palestinian children would be watching.

I tapped my fingers on the desk, waiting for that midnight magic to kick in. But it did not, so eventually, I called it a night, vowing to pin Khalil and Yara down and make tomorrow crossover day. We would not leave until we had at least the concepts in place.

Next morning, Khalil and Yara, our writers, Josh, George, and I poured coffees and sat around the kitchen table at our Al Quds office, ready to put the crossovers to bed—however long it took. With just a couple of weeks of filming left, we had no choice but to get the crossovers written. We were not going to leave the room until we had finalized the three scripts. We could not.

"The thing is," added Yara, "the politics of this is one thing, but we have more fundamental problems here: Our whole show is in Arabic, and the Israeli segments are in Hebrew. There's no reason for our Muppets to speak Hebrew, or the Israeli Muppets to speak Arabic. And why on earth would either group of children go to the other's area? This is really difficult."

But her ability to accept reality and just get it done struck again: "To keep the experience real for our audience," said Yara, "our Muppets can't speak Hebrew. Karim represents a six-year-old Palestinian boy and Hanin, a four-year-old girl, why would they speak any language other than their mother tongue? We can't use subtitles for obvious reasons, and dubbing would be even weirder. I guess, first, we need to figure out a translator, someone to bridge between the two languages and the two cultures."

At that moment, the cast jostled their way into the office for an early-morning read-through. At the back of the group, Hussam Abu Eisheh walked and chatted with Rajai Sandouka, our Muppeteer for Karim.

"Of course! How had I missed it? Hussam learned to speak Hebrew when he served time in an Israeli jail. He can be the translator in his role as Ustaz Adel. He would be perfect."

Stumbling across the 'who' was a start, but working out the 'how' remained a complete mystery.

Our first hurdle was to overcome the language barrier. We knew using Ustaz the music teacher as a translator would work, and we had one of the Israeli human characters, the Palestinian—Israeli doctor, available to help us bridge the language gap on their street. But still the problem hung in the air: When and why would the Israeli Muppets visit *Shara'a Simsim*?

While we had seen the problem with Israelis being in Palestinian territory first hand, the Americans and Israelis felt that the difficulties should not affect the children's program: The Muppets would simply appear on the set. As far as they were concerned, there was no need to explain to the audience how they got there.

"Israelis don't just appear on Palestinian streets unless they are settlers. How on earth are we going to tackle this?" I said in one angry outburst.

Josh stepped into the silence to help us find a solution: "*Sesame Street* scripts always have two prerequisites: They need to be educational, and they need to be entertaining. If either of these pillars is weak, the script usually fails. Look at the curriculum document—what educational goals could we go for? We don't need to write the scripts now—just get the premise in place. Once we have those sorted, we can look at making them funny later."

"Hmm. Well, maybe Dr. Amal from the Israeli street is Ustaz Adel's cousin," Khalil suggested.

"And maybe to bring the two together, we could have Amal visit for Ustaz Adel's birthday party," I said.

"...she brings a friend from *Rehov Sumsum* with her," offered Josh.

The basic idea worked, but what would they do?

Remembering the discussion in Tiberias, one of the few times we had brainstormed with the Israelis, I made a suggestion: "Listen, we know the Israelis like to claim falafel, pita and hummus as theirs, but maybe we could play into that. Dr. Amal could bring some falafel with her, and Adel could be preparing some hummus."

For years, Palestinians have been complaining that Israelis are stealing cultural symbols and claiming them for their own. American Jewish restaurants in New York have signs that sell 'Israeli' falafel. An image of an Israeli EL AL flight attendant wearing the traditional Palestinian embroidered dress was criticized in the local press, who said it was another sign that Israelis were trying to steal Palestinian culture and folklore, and portray it as Israeli. But maybe Ayman had a point.

"My worry," George said, "is that it might legitimize the Israeli attempt to steal our folklore and favorite foods, contradicting our aim to represent and to portray pride in Palestinian culture for the next generation. But this was never going to be easy!"

Yara Jalajel, our fourteen-year-old superstar script writer, came up with an idea: "Since Israelis and Palestinians both know falafel and hummus, why don't the Muppets talk to each other with various versions of 'hummus' and 'falafel?'"

She started trying it out: "Hummus hummus, falafel hummus, falafel falafel." She mimicked the Muppet brilliantly. Simple yet profound.

We tried to maintain our role of responsible, serious adults, but we could not help but crack a smile, and then, as Yara's mono-dialog continued, we laughed out loud, and we agreed we could live with the sharing of these two chickpea-based foods, for *Sesame Street* at least.

Here was a Palestinian child who could do what the adults, despite all our learning and experience, had failed to do. With simplicity, and without trying to create a sophisticated dialog, she had bridged the language gap in a way that fitted Muppet talk and was understood by children and adults on both sides.

Sorting one of the crossovers out really helped Khalil's creativity and imagination. He quickly came up with a second credible setting, while both sticking to the Sesame New York pedagogic curriculum and introducing the Israeli and Palestinian Muppets.

"How about an Israeli child goes out for a ride on his bike," Khalil started. "Say he takes a wrong turn and gets lost and ends up in *Shara'a Simsim* ... maybe he gets a flat tire in this strange and unfamiliar street," he suggested.

It had the beginnings of a perfect *Sesame Street* episode.

"When Karim and Hanin see the little boy, they try hard to rescue their new-found Israeli friend and go on a hunt to bring him a replacement tire," Khalil started to flesh out his idea.

"As they look at the flat bicycle tire, Karim and Hanin speak to each other in Arabic and gesture to the Israeli boy."

The Muppets would use the familiar Arabic *banchar*, which possibly derives from the English word 'puncture,' to tell each other and the audience that they need to help this Israeli boy.

Catching on quickly as ever, Yara added: "They look at him and say in Arabic, with gestures, 'Stay here! We will be right back.'"

"Karim reappears, pleased as punch, holding a very small tire," continues Khalil. "The Israeli boy looks, puzzled, at the tire, and rejects it politely: 'Too small' he says in Hebrew and hand gestures. 'Too small,' Karim agrees with the boy, and then tells Hanin: 'Too small.' Karim quickly tells the Israeli boy again: 'Please wait here! We will be right back.' Moments later, again Karim returns, really happy with himself, this time holding a huge tire. 'Way too big,' says the Israeli boy in Hebrew and gestures, which Karim translates for Hanin. The Muppets nod at each other and disappear as the Israeli boy waits. Finally, Karim brings the right-sized bicycle tire for the Israeli boy, who cycles away happily waving to his new Palestinian friends." Khalil was on a roll, and it was wonderful to watch his creative mind throw ideas out, piling one on top of the other.

Months later, after filming and editing, when the Sesame educators saw it, they were happy that we were teaching children the differences between small and large as well as contributing to solving the decades-old Arab—Israeli conflict.

But when Palestinians saw the bicycle crossover, there was quite a reaction. People found symbolism in the tire sizes, saying they reflected the different negotiation offers that had appeared during the peace process, and there were suggestions we were pushing for a pragmatic solution based on a centralized and moderate land offer.

As a life-long active left-wing nationalist, Khalil would not have considered this as he wrote the script. His family in Jerusalem has suffered much under the Israelis, and to accuse him of writing a script that represented political kowtowing was unfair and unjust.

With two scripts down and one to go, we were doing well. But the third script proved harder than we expected. We needed just one more funny sketch that pulled Israeli and Palestinian children together. I thought we could play with the idea of using a common enemy to show each group that, although the grown-ups were fighting and seemed to not like the other, children could find common ground.

"Maybe we should figure out something that can unite children. What we need is something they all agree that they don't like," I said.

For hours, we hemmed and hawed; we threw ideas into a pit of useless sketches, and we were about to give up without an answer, and call it a day, when the office phone rang. My ten-year-old daughter was on the line and wanted to know when I was coming home.

"We're very nearly finished, Tamara. I'll be home soon enough. In fact, maybe you can help us out, and I'll get home earlier: Can you tell me something all children hate?"

"Dad, that's easy. We all hate onions."

"That's it! You're brilliant! I'll be home soon."

I went back to the team with this breaking news. George, who is technically an Israeli citizen from the town of Nazareth and is fluent in Hebrew, told us that the words for 'onion' in Arabic and Hebrew are similar.

We took a while to work out the punchline, but when we found it, the rest of the crossover fell into place. With punchline in hand, we worked backwards to build the dramatic set up. We had to create a situation with a problem, then one or two attempts to resolve it before ending up with our prepared zinger.

It was close to four in the afternoon, and we had achieved more than I had even dared to hope we would the night before with that blank screen staring back at me. We had eaten a mountain of food and drunk gallons of coffee and tea, and we had two convincing crossover sketches. All that was left to do was come up with an item that unified Palestinian and Israeli children against onions.

"The scene starts with a visit to *Shara'a Simsim* from *Rehov Sumsum*'s Muppets and children," suggested George. "They all play and chat side-by-side in their own languages, as only children can, but are clearly tired and hungry. After making a tour of the Street—you know, to introduce the Israelis to the Palestinian Street—they end up at Im Nabil's home. Im Nabil calls the children in to eat:

'I've prepared for you a hot dish of *musakhan* chicken.'"

Musakhan is one of Palestine's national dishes, made of chicken cooked with onions and seasoned with *sumak* spice (not the poisonous *sumac*) and is served with bread baked in special *taboon* ovens, where the dough is laid on very hot stones, which cook from beneath, producing loaves of bread that have small hills and valleys. When I was at Messiah College in the U.S., at the tender age of sixteen, my mom sent me off with nearly a freezer full of musakhan chicken, so I could tuck in when I needed a taste of home. Hungry, I would heat it up in the dorm kitchen, filling the dorm with its glorious aroma. It did not take long for other students to gravitate to the kitchen, eager to see what I was eating. They joined me at the table, and we would share the musakhan, which they renamed Arab chicken. Whenever they hit a low point or needed some comfort food, they would ask when we could have Arab chicken again—it was something to cheer them up.

Like my old dorm friends, the children in the crossover sketch salivate, full of expectation as they watch the hot chicken carried by Im Nabil. Then she delivers the face turner:

"I made you this delicious *musakhan*, children, with lots of *basal* [onions]."

"*Basal?*" says the Palestinian Muppet.

"*Batzal?*" says the Israeli Muppet.

All children and the Muppets scream at the thought of onions, and the scene ends with a zinger.

As the final elements of the narrative fall into place, a tired cheer goes up around the table. We did it. We managed to come up with three crossover segments. What a day! Wearing tired smiles, we wished each other a good evening—*masa' al-khair*—and made our way home.

By the next day, Yara and Khalil had worked their magic, following the *Sesame Street* script formula: Create a problem, make two attempts to resolve it, and then find the solution, followed up with a musical jingle that identifies resolution.

In the nick of time, I took the three new scripts to Tel Aviv, so we could film the crossovers in the final couple of weeks of shooting. Aware of how difficult we had found the crossovers, politically and conceptually, the Israelis were incredibly supportive. While they had created enough crossover segments in which the Palestinian characters speak Arabic, and the Israeli kids speak Hebrew to have one in almost all of their thirty-minute programs, our fifteen-minute show had three, and we kept Hebrew to a bare minimum. Nonetheless, filmed over just a couple of days, the crossovers ended up being successful, forging further bonds between the teams.

Yara's 'Hummus! Falafel! Hummus!' segment was the last segment to be filmed in Tel Aviv, in what was, by then, a warm, pleasant atmosphere. Watching Hanin and Dafi, the Israeli monster, squeal as they become friends, discovering they love some of the same foods, everyone laughed so much that we had to re-tape the segment. Seeing grins on the faces of every actor and crew member on that last day, I gathered everyone around for a 'wrap' photo—but instead of everyone shouting the normal 'cheeeeeeeessssse,' I suggested something a bit more topical. Everyone called 'falafeeeeeeeeeel,' and we got a wonderful group photo of smiling Israelis and Palestinians, side by side.

Arrest and Hunger Strike

AFTER TWO YEARS OF PLANNING and scriptwriting, breaking down barriers, fundraising, and filming interspersed with awkward meetings with the Israelis, on April 1, 1997, my birthday, cast, crew, and Lewis, who flew in from New York for the happy occasion, squeezed in front of cheap TV sets at Al Quds Educational TV HQ and settled in to watch *Sesame Street* broadcast for the first time. Seeing our hard work on screen, all the effort, all the anguish, made sense. What a great birthday present! I was on top of the world, but it was not going to last.

Over the previous year, while Star2000 and the team worked on post-production, I turned my attention to building Al Quds Educational Television. On January 20, 1996, Palestinians went to the voting stations for the first Palestinian Legislative Council (PLC) elections, the result of the 1993 Oslo Agreement ratified on the White House Lawn between the Palestinian leader, Yasser Arafat, and Israel's Yitzhak Rabin.

My brother, Jonathan (Atallah), ran for the Jerusalem Christian seat, and when the results were announced, we were told that we had lost the elections by a few hundred votes; rumors of rigging were flying around, but the possibility of electoral fraud did not faze me. My spirits were not dampened. Although the elections did not mean complete freedom for Palestinians, even if it did mean the withdrawal of the Israeli Army from populated cities, I saw them as part of a peace process that would result, in time, in independence for the Palestinian people.

Young and full of idealism, I was so excited about the future that I failed to question whether we were moving in a true democracy, but nothing was going to stop me from joining the liberation process.

While Palestinian Basic Law provided for a presidential government (as is the case in all Arab countries), I truly believed that the freely elected parliament would provide for a strong legislative branch of government. For my part, I wanted to elevate the Palestinian people's voice using television. As the Director of the year-old public-service television station associated with Al Quds University, and in anticipation of the first airing of *Shara'a Simsim*, I felt I should use my position to support and advance the political process. I leapt into raising public awareness about the workings of the newly elected parliament; I knew that I had a lot to learn, and that I was walking into unknown territory, but the idea of being part of a national movement in the temporary Palestinian capital, Ramallah, energized me.

In addition to the children's *Shara'a Simsim*, I applied for permission to air C-SPAN–like broadcasts of the Palestinian Legislative Council. I contacted the Palestinian parliament speaker and the architect of the Oslo Accords, Ahmad Qurei, (Abu Ala'a), whom I eventually convinced, but it was not easy. He was not exactly opposed to the idea, but he thought filming excerpts and broadcasting a shorter version at night, or once a week, would make more sense. I knew enough about Arab politics and journalism to know that this would be a formula for self-censorship. So many politicians and other powers-that-be in the Arab world use this trick as powerful intimidation. Instead of practicing direct control, they often use their powers to get journalists to do their censorship or editing for them. Knowing that anything short of a live unedited program would inevitably result in pressure on my staff, I asked politely but firmly for the right to broadcast the sessions—live—and he agreed.

While *Sesame Street* was in post-production at Star2000, we set up some new small cameras in the makeshift parliament in the auditorium of a local Ramallah high school, and we began to broadcast the sessions in March 1997. Before long, though, we started to get some negative feedback from people close the Palestinian president. I ignored the critique in the belief that the broadcasts were for the national good. Not much later, we noticed some interference and began to see a square black frame superimposed on our broadcasts. I assumed the interference was related to the earlier negative comments emerging from Arafat's inner circle, so I raised the issue with the speaker of the Palestinian Legislative Council. During a break in one of the sessions, I simply approached the podium, and I told Abu Ala'a what was happening. He was livid.

"You keep broadcasting." He told me, almost as a patriotic order, "And if you have to record and distribute these tapes on the black market, do it."

I made sure that members of the parliament found out about the jamming and one of them, Hatem Abdel Qader, a former colleague of mine at the pro-PLO daily *Al Fajr*, made public our predicament during the next session and insisted the parliament's secretariat do something about it. I also called up a few foreign journalists to entice them to do a story, but, really, I gave up believing the jamming would end.

Instead we found ways to bypass it. As Abu Ala'a suggested, we simply made copies of televised sessions and distributed tapes to local television stations in Nablus, Tulkarm, Jenin, Bethlehem, Hebron, and Ramallah, who broadcast it unedited to excited audiences. I did not realize it then, but we made our position even more precarious, pushing the local authorities to use more extreme approaches to stop us.

The interference continued for some time. But things changed dramatically one day early in May. As I walked into the studio on May 19, our engineer, Ayman Noor, greeted me with the news we had been waiting and working for.

Exhilarated, I went to the council chamber and approached several key deputies. "The jamming has stopped," I said. Surprised, the deputies reasoned that perhaps their efforts to gain freedom of the press had, in fact, been successful. Marwan Barghouti, head of the West Bank branch of the Fatah National Liberation Movement, President Arafat's mainstream guerrilla movement, said the jamming issue had been raised the night before in a meeting with President Arafat: "Maybe that's the reason the jamming stopped."

That day, I walked away feeling gratified. In the belief that we had won a significant battle, I enthused during my journalism lecture that afternoon: "Freedom of expression is something that has to be won; we can't take it for granted," I preached. "Journalists often have to make sacrifices to get and keep this freedom; they might even have to fight laws and traditions in pursuit of freedom of expression." Little did I know, within a few hours, my ideals would be put to the test.

From our relatively free-and-fair Palestinian elections, independent parliamentarians willing to challenge the executive authority started to appear, and, that evening, with the jamming stopped, the country saw a compelling session about the Palestinian Authority's annual budget. Legislative MP Rawia Shawwa, a tough woman from Gaza with perfectly arranged hair and stylish dress, attacked the idea of monopolies being established by the Palestinian Authority. Parliamentary powers were rather new to our region and some members of the legislature enjoyed their privileges a little too much. Shawwa and other delegates addressed the concern that some government officials and ministers had two or three homes, and that cars were provided not only for officials but for their family members as well. In one heated exchange, some ministers' names were entered into the discussion to add credibility to the charge—and all this was aired by a local broadcaster courageous (or stupid) enough to publicize words without filters or censors, and without attempting to appease the office of the president.

In many countries, what I was doing would be considered a normal act of an independent media, but in our region—where self-censorship is the rule rather than the exception—my actions in publicizing the corruption of the Palestinian Authority was nothing short of reckless. In a region where the head of the tribe (or country) rules without question, what I was attempting to do was borderline revolutionary, and not in the good way.

Throughout the evening, friends across the West Bank called me, delighted to be able to see and hear such open and hard-hitting discussions about the budget. With each call came the reassurance that the jamming had stopped.

Thrilled by the day's developments, I began to get ready for bed, then at around 11 p.m., the phone rang. My thirty-eight-year-old wife, Nuha, in an incurable stage of her fight with breast cancer, looked up,

"Don't answer it. You've been on the phone all evening." The phone rang out, then it started again immediately, and again. My natural journalistic curiosity got the better of me. I picked up the phone.

"This is Captain Ali Ghneim from the Ramallah police investigation unit. Could you kindly come down for a cup of coffee?"

"Does it concern the television station?"

"No," he lied, "just come."

"Can it wait until tomorrow, or do you want me right away?"

"It is best if you come now."

"Can I bring a lawyer with me?"

"Sure, whoever you want."

As I pulled on jeans and shoes without socks (not expecting to stay too long), I called my brother, Jonathan, an attorney. Jonathan asked me to pick him up on the way to the station. Regardless of Captain Ali Ghneim's comments, I worried that the late-night call was connected to the television work, so I called Imad Abu-Kishek, Director of Public Relations at Al Quds University.

Al Quds University owns the TV station, and Imad, an activist with the PLO since his student days, had many connections with Palestinian security, so I felt he ought to be informed. He suggested I pick him up instead of dragging Jonathan along.

Colonel Ghneim met us as we arrived at the Central Police Station in Ramallah. "You came very quickly."

"I have nothing to hide."

We sat. Imad and the colonel (both tested fighters and belonging to the same Fatah PLO faction) eyed each other, trying to figure out what the other was thinking. If there was any difference between them, it was that Imad was among the local fighters born and raised in Palestine, while the colonel was born to a Palestinian family abroad and joined the PLO when Arafat returned to Palestine.

Finally, Colonel Ghneim spoke directly to me.

"Are you connected to the Al Quds University Educational Television Station?" he asked.

"Yes!" It was the only direct and relevant question I was asked.

Imad interjected, "Anything you have to say about the station should be directed to me. I am the official representative of the university."

The colonel ignored him. He turned again to me: "I'd like you to wait in the next room." I was ushered into an adjoining room and my cell phone was taken away; Imad was taken out of the office.

While I waited at the police station, Jonathan, who realized that it was not going to be a short visit, came by around 2:30 a.m., and we were allowed to meet. Once together, I made an important decision. There were so many cases of people told to keep their arrest out of the public eye then left to rot in jail, and I didn't want to take that route: "Don't hesitate for a second. Don't just wait to see if this can be resolved behind the scenes; get this out to as many news agencies as you can."

For the next hour, I talked to every police officer who accidently opened the door of the administration room I was held in. I demanded that the police either charge or release me. When demanding failed, I tried a personal, humanitarian request.

"My wife is very ill," I told every officer that went by, "I can't be away from her very long."

I persisted with my plea until one of the officers allowed me to call my ailing wife. "We're just waiting for a phone call, then you'll be released," he told me, justifying my call home.

No phone call came. At 4:30 a.m., a mattress and a piece of foam to serve as pillow or blanket was dumped on the floor of the administration room, and the door locked from the outside. Exhausted, I fell asleep.

I woke at 7:30 a.m., just as the first police officer arrived for the day shift. It was Aisha, a young police officer from Ramallah. Aisha, it turned out, had been active in the intifada and, after it, joined the police where she was assigned to computer work, mostly typing up reports written by other police. While she worked, I walked around the computer room to pass time and read the memos on the bulletin board. Two caught my attention. One: A note about limiting the number of officers allowed to accompany senior police or military officials, and the names of those given this privilege. Two: A memo telling of the punishment of a Ramallah police officer who had beaten a local citizen with a sharp object. The officer had been given one month in jail and deducted one month's salary for his brutality. I was impressed.

"Incidents like this should be reported," I mentioned to Aisha, "Telling people about the punishment of a police officer would do a great deal to improve the image of the Palestinian Security Forces."

No one would tell me what my status was, so, by 9 a.m., I decided to act. I made my first demand. "I'd like to have breakfast," I said. One of the police officers brought five pieces of *kmaj* (pita bread), and three hard-boiled eggs. No plate, no utensils, no tray, no salt—just bread and eggs.

As I ate, my family, the press, and the staff members from the U.S. Consulate fought to find out where I was. Because I am a U.S. citizen and because the controversial *Sesame Street* broadcasting project and our media institute was U.S. funded, the consulate played an active role in the search. The Palestinian police told anyone asking about my status that they did not know where I was, that I had left the police station the previous night.

A close friend at the U.S. Consulate, Samir Rantisi, (now deceased) refused to buy the lies; he insisted that I had not returned home and was last seen in the police station. Trying to get out of it, Colonel Ghneim tried to mislead him:

"He's probably off spending the night with a woman."

Furious by the allegation, Samir doubled his efforts. Meanwhile, I busied myself reading a book my brother brought me the day before. All day, I was guarded by Mohammed, a young policeman from Gaza, transferred to Ramallah for striking a fellow officer. He had been demoted and was very unhappy with the world. Mohammad watched me read *Bloomberg by Bloomberg*, the autobiography of a man who made millions by creating a unique communication tool for stock information. Mohammad interrupted my reading:

"Aren't you bored of reading?"

I wanted to ask him if he was illiterate, but instead I replied: "I read because I am bored."

By the afternoon, Samir succeeded. I was 'officially' in the police station, and U.S. Consulate representative Terry Leach was allowed to see me in the police chief's office.

Colonel-General Firas Amleh, a senior officer, greeted me in his upstairs office. "Wouldn't it be nice if all Palestinians were Daoud Kuttab?" he sneered. "I never had as many requests to see a Palestinian as I have for you." Then, in a mark of respect for the U.S. official, Colonel-General Amleh left the office, so I could speak with Terry alone.

While Terry took notes as she asked questions about the police's treatment of me, instinctively, my eyes zoomed in on her pen and yellow legal pad; I saw my diary starting before my eyes.

"Terry, could I have that pen?" I asked. She smiled and handed me both the pen and the pad, finding spares for herself in her briefcase.

Before she left, she gave me a couple of books to read and her card: "Call me anytime if you have a problem!"

Soon, I was back with my host, Mohammed, but this time cradling a pen and a pad, so I settled in to write notes and thoughts in my makeshift diary until another police official came into the room later that day. I wore him down; I fought to see my children the next day. We are such a close family that not seeing them was the cruelest punishment, so when he agreed I would see them in the morning, my tension lifted, and I fell fast asleep.

With restrictions on visits relaxed, on Thursday I had a flood of visitors: some of the staff from the university, the head of the Palestinian Journalists Union, and the U.S. Consul, General Edward Abington. I did not expect that. I also did not know that Secretary of State Madeline Albright was aware of my predicament. Abington promised that he would take up my case with President Arafat as soon as he could: Everyone was just waiting for the president to return from Egypt, and all of this would be cleared up.

Dr. Yaser Abu-Khater from the Independent Commission on Citizen's Rights also stopped by. Together, we succeeded in getting the police chief to tell us why I was being held.

"There has been an order to detain you from none other than President Arafat himself." Colonel-General Amleh confirmed what I'd suspected from the beginning.

"Is the order in writing?"

"No."

"What is the legal status of being restrained?" I pushed, more confident having a human rights' activist present. "How long is the period of restraint? Can I get out on bail for just being 'restrained' and not 'charged' with a crime?"

"Only the person who ordered the restraint can order the release. This will all be settled when you meet with the president. He's expected back in Ramallah anytime." And, at that, the colonel turned away, unwilling to say more.

Amused, I replied, "Why didn't you tell me I'd be seeing President Arafat? I would have worn socks and dressed for the occasion."

An officer ushered me away from Colonel-General Amleh and back to my admin-room prison, but the previously empty room, cleared by the police to give us some privacy, now rang with the cheers of my beautiful children. My detention felt much better with them there, and I joked with them, trying to put them at ease and help them feel OK about my detention.

"Once I meet with President Arafat, and he releases me, I will ask for an appointment and take you all to see him, and you can have your picture taken with him," I laughed. Tamara glared at me, her body language screaming "No way." I steered clear of my detention for the rest of the visit, and instead listened to their babbles about home.

As I watched them leave, I was sad both to see them go, and for the situation they had to get their heads around. Maybe being arrested for my beliefs by Palestine's enemies would have been easier for them to understand; being held by my own country was incomprehensible for my children, who grew up believing that Arafat and the PLO were the good guys: What should my children think of their own Palestinian Authority, a government our people fought so hard to get? Where was the better life they had been promised; the rights the authority swore to defend for us? There I was in a Palestinian jail with no charge against me. An Israeli prison would have made this a political problem. An easier notion for their minds to process.

Winding myself up with negative thoughts was not healthy, so I ate the hummus and a couple pieces of pita bread brought in on a chipped plate by the police officer and decided to push the thoughts aside and concentrate on their next visit the following morning. Friday in Palestine is the weekend. I would keep the next day's jokes nonpolitical, I decided as I drifted off to sleep.

At 10 a.m., a commotion in the outer office woke me. I sat up in anticipation, expecting the children. I opened the unlocked door, and, sure enough, I saw my children with my sister-in-law, Beth. Without warning, though, the children were ushered out of the corridor, leaving me with only a glimpse of them and giving them only a glimpse of me. No explanation given. Frantic, I called to the officer to find out what was happening, but I was ignored. (Later, I discovered that a CNN crew had followed the children into the police station. A police officer had stuck his hand over the camera lens and called a stop to the intended visit.) I looked out the window and saw banks of journalists, including CNN's Jerrold Kessel and his crew. Without a lot of thought,

I decided to begin a hunger strike. With my U.S. Consulate pad and pen, I scribbled the words 'Hunger Strike' in English and in Arabic and whistled to the CNN cameraman to film in my direction.

The CNN crew noticed me, and I saw the photographer trying to zoom in on the piece of paper. Within moments, an officer realized I was communicating with the outside world and stormed into the room, so I dropped the paper from the window to the street below.

When the police chief learned of my hunger strike, he had me bundled and sent upstairs where my confidence about the injustice of my detention was confirmed—the prison chief tried to bully me into giving up my hunger strike.

"No way," I told him straight, "I will eat only in my own house."

Being on hunger strike gave me power. Every time food, tea, or coffee appeared, I rejected it and felt stronger. As a prisoner, I demanded and was allowed to see the local newspaper *Al Quds*. I'd been told that there was no mention of my arrest in the paper until that issue, which ran a quote from Imad Abu-Kishek, the public relations officer from Al-Quds University: The university had decided to suspend all broadcasts of the Legislative Council sessions, clearly wanting to lower the tension and give the leadership in Gaza a chance to come down from the tree they had climbed, and I accepted this compromise as necessary for my release, and given my wife's terminal condition, I wanted to get out as soon as possible. Sari Nusseibeh, the president of Al Quds University, obviously had one thing in mind: to get me, a university employee, out of jail. Maybe shutting down the broadcasts was part of a deal for my release. I felt upbeat, and when the police chief told me to collect my belongings, I was convinced I was going home. No such luck.

Loaded into a jeep, I learned home was not my destination; the central prison in the Palestinian Authorities headquarters, commonly referred to as *muqataa*, was making me a certified prisoner.

On Sunday, May 25, 1997, I woke up in a cell in the central prison at the Palestinian Authority's headquarters, a long way from the admin room at the police station in Ramallah. The three-by-four-meter box-like room had a metal door and a small waist-height window, which was the only real source of light. Hearing my stomach growl, I squatted to see through the window and squinted at prisoners taking their morning exercise in the *fora*—the tiled yard. As my eyes adjusted, I noticed prisoner after prisoner looking back at me through the window. I felt like a monkey in a zoo, and I was on edge. One prisoner, a total stranger to me, surprised me and called me by name:

"Daoud! Your story has been all over the news; I'm sure you'll be released, soon," he said.

At 11 a.m., the prisoners returned to their cells, and the guards let me out to walk around. One of the guards rushed towards me, telling me that one of his neighbors, a colleague of mine from the university, asked him to find me to see if I needed anything.

Immediately, I thought of Nuha. "Can you send a message to my wife and tell her where I am, and that I'm fine?"

"I wish I could," he whispered.

My heart dropped.

"OK," he looked around, "give me your phone number."

I scribbled a message on a scrap of paper from my U.S. Consulate yellow pad, and then signed it. I added my home phone number and my brother's phone number and hoped for the best. Getting it to my family had to work. They needed to know I was safe. My friend Hanan Ashrawi lived close to the prison, and I knew I could trust her to contact Nuha and the children. My note only needed to get to her house, then Hanan or her husband, Emile (whose sister is married to a Kuttab), could call my family.

At 3:30 p.m., from the radio down the corridor came exciting news: A report saying that the U.S. Consul-General Ed Abington had met with President Arafat and pleaded for my release.

Convinced I would be free by evening, when a guard passed by, I asked to take a shower. The police officers' bathroom water was cold, but I showered, preparing for my inevitable release. My anxiety lessened.

But nothing happened. The afternoon and early evening passed uneventfully, just a headache from low sugar to keep me company, mainly punctuated by pangs of hunger and waves of mild nausea.

At midnight, my cell door opened and four policemen, dressed in light-blue uniforms marking them as members of Palestinian Special Police, entered my cell. My detention was over, surely. But quick as they appeared, they left. Something felt wrong, and the hunger that was eating my stomach also increased my fear.

At 11:40 a.m. the next day, again a guard appeared, this one, though, let me out for a walk around in the *fora*. Part of me still believed I would soon be released. But that was not the plan: They wanted to test me, to challenge my hunger strike. Lunch—lentils and rice with onions and salad on top—was laid before me, and I really wanted it, really wanted to sink my teeth into it. But my hunger strike, my freedom, was more important than any meal. I turned away and hardened my resolve. My hunger strike had a purpose, a principle.

Escorted back to my cell, depressed, I questioned everything: Why was I still in jail? What had changed? Maybe it was the American pressure. To motivate the peace process over the previous few months, the Palestinian Authority had demanded ever more U.S. involvement, but would probably resent any American pressure to help me.

The guard who took my messages the previous day caught me and told me he would send out my mail when the visitors came for their regular weekly meetings. A wave of nausea hit as I realized Nuha and the children had not heard from me since I left the police station. My thoughts drifted to another prisoner I had met who had been in prison for ten months without charge. Would I be left that long? For me, it would be a struggle, but I could cope, but what about my wife and children? Their punishment felt worse than mine—they should not have to go through it.

With my one possession, my pen, as the sun set on day two, I scrawled a letter to President Arafat exclaiming my innocence. I told him that in broadcasting the sessions, I had acted within the law. I told him that our station had a broadcasting license from his own Information Ministry, and I told him we had a formal contract with the Legislative Council to broadcast their sessions live. I appealed to him on humanitarian grounds: I told him that Nuha was sick and needed me with her. I poured my predicament on to the paper. Writing was cathartic; it fed my hope.

I called the guard and asked to speak to the warden.

"The warden is asleep."

My hunger made me fidget and made me angry. The energy I used on being angry made me hungrier, and I had all but given up. How could I get my letter to President Arafat if the warden would not see me?

My body would not let me pace the room; it would not let me walk. I just lay on the cot, staring at shapes on the wall, feeling the heat of day three rise. The guards left boiled eggs, pita, and a carton of mango juice next to my mattress, taunting me, and it took all the willpower and energy I had to turn away from it.

By afternoon, the warden finally bustled in, took the letter from me with a promise to send it immediately, and left. And I was alone again, but my hungry light-headedness began to fade as I lay there.

Time passed, how much I could not say, and the warden returned with a doctor who tried to convince me to stop my hunger strike. I refused and realized I was beginning to feel a little better—maybe my body was adjusting to my new diet.

"Just do your job," I said.

But, the doctor's serious look worried me. Hunger strike is a physically violent, fatally dangerous non-violent mode of protest. Was my feeling better a signal that I was getting worse? That my body was shutting down? What hunger does to the body is horrific: Hallucinations and dementia start around three weeks; after four weeks, the body starts to consume itself; and from five weeks, damage to the brain and internal organs can be permanent. During the first three days of my hunger strike, I had never felt as sick in my life. But something had happened at the end of day three. When the doctor collected his things, and the men began to leave, I struggled to my feet to stop the warden.

"I'd like to talk to you alone."

The warden told the doctor to go on.

"I know you want me to end my hunger strike," I said. "How about a compromise? You let me call my wife—no one has to know—and I will drink tea with you. You can take the credit for convincing me to stop. It has to be a deal between you and me, though."

"I will be happy to ask for permission for you to call your wife," he said. Clearly, the deal was a no-go. I slumped to the mattress, and he left.

The next three days merged into each other. Food and a carton of mango juice was left by my mattress every morning, and every morning, I ignored it—which became easier each day. Walks around the *fora* punctuated hours of sitting on the mattress in my cell, thinking about home. Sometimes I snatched discussions with other prisoners or guards, and other times I was able to hear the news on the guards' radio.

At seven on the sixth evening, I was pushed into the courtyard, yet again, to trudge around for twenty minutes, despondent, until a guard ordered me to return to my cell.

"Why?"

"Orders from the warden."

On my stumble back to the cell, guards passed me, carrying several large plastic containers of milk. My heart and my head raced. They were preparing a milk and egg-yolk mix to force-feed me. I was afraid. Would I resist? Would I glug the milk-and-egg mixture without a fight? I had an idea: the mango juice. I would not let them win. I would break my fast before they could do it for me.

In my cell, I grabbed the juice, pierced it with my pen, and guzzled the sweet juice. The door creaked open, and I stumbled to the far end of the cell to stash the half-empty juice box. The warden and a number of Special Forces Police in their blue uniforms and polished style strode in and filled the room. I was ready to resist: The mango juice hardened my resolve.

"Put on some clothes," the warden said.

"Where are we going?" In my fear, all I could think was that they were going to take me elsewhere to force-feed me. Let's just get on with it!

"Just put on your clothes," the warden repeated.

My prisoner shorts fell to the hard floor, and I pulled on my jeans and my shoes. The rest of my clothes, my books, letters from prisoners, and the hidden mango-juice box remained behind. We marched to the end of the prison and got into a jeep. We drove along bumpy roads back to the Central Police Station in Ramallah, where I had been for 'just a cup of coffee' seven nights before.

Confused and hiding my hope, I assumed we were going to meet with someone from the U.S. Consulate, or maybe even my lawyer, surely not my family. I could not allow the idea of release to enter my mind. It was just another trick.

We entered the police chief's office while he was on the phone.

"Yes, Mr. Kuttab is here," Captain Ghneim, said into the phone. He handed me the phone.

"*Marhaba?*"

"This is General Ghazi Jabali, Chief of the Palestinian police. We received your letter and have decided to release you. You will be confronted by many journalists. Don't say anything provocative," he threatened.

I said only, "You did me wrong. I shouldn't have been in prison."

"We'll talk about that later," he told me. "Just go home and be careful about what you say to the press." The line went dead.

"May I call my wife?" I asked Captain Ghneim.

"Just a second, first you need to sign a declaration."

He drafted a statement in which I agreed to respect the laws of the Palestinian Authority. I scanned it and scrawled my signature across the bottom of the page. I knew it was meaningless: It was scribbled on an unofficial piece of paper. Besides, I could sign the statement in good faith because I had always wanted to respect the laws of the Palestinian Authority. I just wanted the laws of the Palestinian Authority to be based on democracy and justice. The statement did not mention democracy or justice.

A prison guard appeared with my cell phone and the rest of my belongings just as my brother, Jonathan, arrived, in time to see my silent reaction the police chief's repeated warning about talking to the press.

"You didn't respond," said the police chief.

"I heard you," I said simply.

Jonathan leapt to my defense and tried to argue with the police chief. I waved him off; I just wanted to go home.

Hearing Nuha answer the phone weakened and strengthened me. "Heat up some soup for me," and I heard her smile when she realized I was going home.

Seven long days, but in the end, I had won. When I spoke with George Khleifi a few days later, he told me he had called Lewis and the Children's' Television Workshop to let them know I was free.

"What a relief," Lewis had said. And the line went quiet for a moment: "Did they, er … did they torture him?"

George chuckled: "Yes, they took away his cell phone." And in one sentence lightened the situation and reminded Lewis and the American office that Palestinians are not barbarians and do not torture everyone the imprison.

My hunger strike, though, was nothing compared to the hundreds whose only hope is to protest with hunger. When, in 2012, Palestinian prisoners went on hunger strike to protest the continued Israeli administrative detention of hundreds of Palestinians held without charge or trial, I did what I could to bring international focus to their cause by writing and daily tweeting their struggle.

I could do that because my seven-day hunger strike had an enormous effect on my life. I learned so much both about myself and about the internal workings of the Palestinian Authority, and my career went to places I never believed possible.

For days, weeks, and years my story lingered in the media. In addition to the press attention, the French foreign ministry issued a statement; the White House spokesman, Mick McCurry (who I later met to thank), publicly called for my release; and *The Washington Post* ran an editorial defending me and my efforts on behalf of Palestinian press freedom.

In the coming months, with help from the American NGO Internews, USAID provided a major grant to support Palestinian media in training television practitioners and supporting them with equipment. The local newspaper coverage of parliament became much more courageous than before, and our cameras went back to film the Palestinian parliamentary sessions, which, years later, I learned were the first C-SPAN-like broadcasts of any parliament in the entire Arab world.

Thanks to the international pressure, I could be with Nuha when she died—a freedom so many hunger strikers never get—and as we slowly began to heal as a family after we lost Nuha, I could not ignore my fervor and passion inspired by the international support I received during my confinement.

For Nuha, for my children, and for the children of Palestine, I decided to use the recognition I had gained in prison to take *Sesame Street* higher, to get the funding we really needed to help Palestine accept the program as its own. The production crew and I knew if we truly wanted it to be the success it could be, we needed to break away from the Israeli production. And at the end of season one, we took our request to the Jordanians, who stepped in to support us for season two. The budget we needed to keep alive a project the size and quality of

Sesame Street was massive, though, and while Internews, Open Society Institute, and The Ford Foundation helped us enormously in the early days, I needed to get government backing if *Sesame Street* was to have a future.

The following years were filled with overcoming political obstacles and jumping hurdles, but my mission to provide Palestinian children with a world-class, educational, entertaining television program they could be proud of worked. And working with the Americans and the New York-based Sesame Workshop produced the off-screen mutual understanding and respect we were working so hard to instill in our audience. Our children are so much better off today as a result of being exposed to a genuine, local edition of a high-quality global franchise. Said one report:

"Exposure to the program was linked to an increase in children's use of both prosocial justifications to resolve conflicts and positive attributes to describe members of the other group. Palestinian children's abilities to identify symbols of their own culture increased over time. The results indicate the effectiveness of media-based interventions such as *Rechov Sumsum/Shara'a Simsim* on countering negative stereotypes by building a peer-oriented context that introduces children to the everyday lives of people from different cultures." [1]

Children represent the majority of Palestine's population; in fact, they do across the Arab world. Having such a young population, our making sure those formative, preschool years are influenced by a wholesome, entertaining, and educational program could be imperative for future generations.

I am honored to have played a role in bringing *Sesame Street* to Palestine. The journey has been and continues to be rocky yet thrilling. But for the privilege of delivering such exciting children's programming on television, I would not trade it for anything in the world.

---

1. *The educational impact of Rechov Sumsum/Shara'a Simsim: A Sesame Street television series to promote respect and understanding among children living in Israel, the West Bank, and Gaza*, Charlotte F. Cole, Cairo Arafat, Chava Tidhar, Wafa Zidan Tafesh, Nathan A. Fox, Melanie Killen, Alicia Ardila-Rey, Lewis A. Leavitt, Gerry Lesser, Beth A. Richman, Fiona Yung First Published September 1, 2003 Research Article

EPILOGUE: Overcoming Obstacles and Jumping Hurdles

THE PERIOD BETWEEN SEASON TWO and three was perhaps the most difficult. Personally, after coming to terms with Nuha's death, in 1998 I remarried, so the children and I moved to Amman to be with Salam Madanat, my new wife. Politically, the peace process was totally destroyed, and the second intifada erupted. We decided that it was no longer politically feasible to co-produce with the Israelis in any way, so we had to raise our own funds to keep *Sesame Street* alive.

The second intifada was extremely violent, with lots of bloodshed on both sides. And our TV station got up-close-and-personal with it when the Israeli Army decided to re-occupy Ramallah, and, more specifically, for eighteen days, the campus hosting our TV station. They destroyed everything we had built and reminded me sickeningly of seeing a neighbor's home demolished in 1967 when I was taking refuge at my aunt's house in Bethlehem as a boy. Years it took us to rebuild the station, and we were once again invaded and occupied by Israeli forces in 2012 in another attempt to deter us from resisting occupation, but again, it did not. We rebuilt from scratch the shell of our studios they had destroyed.

My American connection has been by my side almost every step of the way. During my many visits to the U.S., to see family, give lectures, and raise funds, I managed to talk with several local American diplomats, who I petitioned to help me convince the U.S. government to financially support *Shara'a Simsim* in the same way they support *Sesame Street* in many parts of the world, including our Egyptian neighbors. It took years of flying back and forth, of meetings and negotiations to convince the American government to support us, and, finally, in 2005, U.S. officials backed us; USAID promised us serious funding, and we had the hope of a secure, successful *Sesame Street* future. But right at that moment, politics overtook all of us.

In January 2006, Islamist pro-Hamas candidates overwhelmingly won the Palestinian parliamentary elections; the U.S. offer of financial aid suddenly evaporated. Even though neither we nor the station were planning to broadcast anything political, the Hamas victory nearly ruined production: The U.S. refused to have any dealings with a people willing to elect Islamic militants to govern.

At the time, I was doing a stint as Ferris Professor of Journalism at Princeton University, putting me just three hours' drive from the USAID offices in Washington and making it relatively easy for me to petition on behalf of the team in Palestine, who managed to produce a mini-series while I was pushing USAID to fulfill its commitments. After many, many visits, two years after the original offer of funding, in 2007 USAID finally came around and agreed to fund two new seasons, allowing us to make children's TV programming and an outreach distribution part of the Palestinian preschool educational policy. The crew back in Palestine was delighted, which pushed me to keep going to see what more we could get. Before my tenure was over, we had secured three more years' USAID funding, which meant the team could start work on fifty-two TV episodes and on putting together a great outreach program to make the series even more real for Palestinian preschoolers.

But in 2010, our journey took us to one of my proudest moments. Not only had we succeeded in becoming a staple on national Palestinian TV, not only had *Shara'a Simsim* become part of the Palestinian Ministry of Education's national five-year strategy, but in September 2010, the Palestinian Prime Minister Salam Fayyad, along with the President of Sesame Workshop Gary Knell (now president of *National Geographic*), as well as the Director of USAID, Howard Sumka, visited our studios in Ramallah as we finally started filming in our own Ramallah-based studio.

Maybe I didn't do very well at school (compared to my older brother Jonathan, who always got straight A's and made his way to the University of Virginia to graduate with a Jurist Doctor—my grade point average did not even reach 3.0), but on that day, hosting so many great people was certainly an overwhelming accomplishment. It was a proud day for me and for our people.

I hung up my boots in 2013, handing daily running of *Shara'a Simsim* over to colleagues Cairo Arafat and Layla Sayegh, allowing me more time to work on publicity, funding and other projects that gave me opportunities to bring the real Palestinian narrative to the world.

Over the years, U.S. private and public funding has come and gone, shifting with the political climate, so I have tried to address our plight through the media, constantly trying to keep *Sesame Street* alive in Palestine, whether through reruns or by sourcing new funding. We clearly need to diversify and look for local Palestinian and Arab backing and not to be totally dependent on one source, especially governmental agencies so easily susceptible to political pressure.

Whether or not we get new funding, and whether or not we produce any new seasons of *Shara'a Simsim*, I feel good about what we have achieved. The programs we produced speak for themselves, and I am excited about all the new talent we helped nurture. Many of our writers, actors, and puppeteers have continued to work in Palestine and throughout the region—and this is a source of pride for all of us.

We Palestinians focused for so long on politics and resistance that we gave up on things like culture, education, and tolerance, but with the help of *Sesame Street*, parents now have culturally relevant content freely available to them. Many of *Shara'a Simsim* songs, segments, and full episodes are available on YouTube, so parents can teach our children not only the alphabet but also life skills, so kids can dream their own dreams and be a part of our collective aspirations.

Everyone involved in *Shara'a Simsim* feels our efforts in early childhood programming has made the possibility of an independent Palestinian state more real. What is even more gratifying, though, is that our children now have a new rhetoric—one where we accomplish our goals non-violently, through tolerance, education, and national pride.

Made in the USA
Monee, IL
05 December 2023